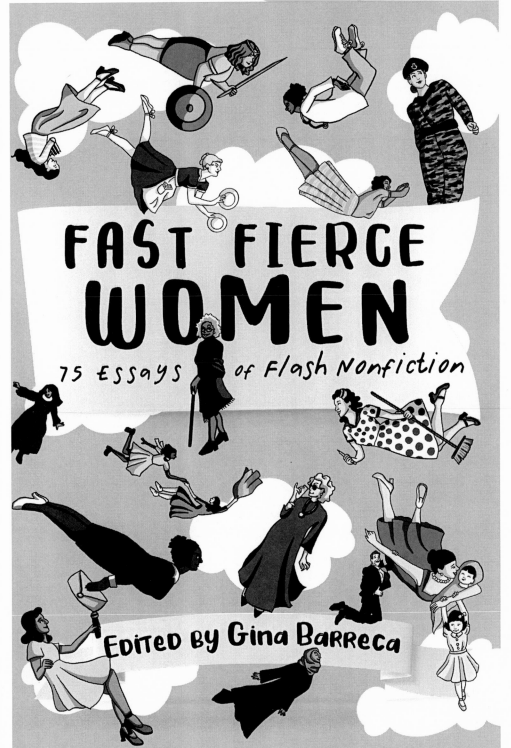

FAST FIERCE WOMEN

75 Essays of Flash Nonfiction

Edited by Gina Barreca

This is a book of flash nonfiction. Each author has created a complete story in 750 or fewer words. Some pieces experiment with form, others take a more traditional approach, but all of them celebrate the precise and concise style of writing that inspired Shakespeare to call brevity the soul of wit.

FAST FIERCE WOMEN

75 Essays of Flash Nonfiction

Edited by Gina Barreca

woodhall press

NORWALK, CONNECTICUT

woodhall press

Woodhall Press, 81 Old Saugatuck Road, Norwalk, CT 06855
WoodhallPress.com

The essay "Rage Begins at Home" reprinted with permission from *The Massachusetts Review*, spring 1993 vol. 34 no. 1.

Cover design: Miranda Wright
Layout artist: Amie McCracken

Library of Congress Cataloging-in-Publication Data available
ISBN 978-1-954907-00-3 (paper: alk paper)
ISBN 978-1-954907-01-0 (electronic)
First Edition

Distributed by Independent Publishers Group
(800) 888-4741
Printed in the United States of America

Contents

GINA BARRECA   *Introduction,* **viii**

CAROLINE LEAVITT   *Dying to Be Better,* **1**

PHILLIS LEVIN   *Secret Rites,* **3**

CHEYENNE SMITH   *As God Is My Witness,* **5**

LARA SCALZI MEEK   *How "Pretty Pretty Princess" Helped Me Find Love, aka Spin Your Way to Romance and Jewelry,* **8**

MAUREEN CORRIGAN   *Fierce Skin,* **10**

NILOUFAR REZAI   *Niloufar Comes to America,* **12**

MIA YANOSY   *The Voice Inside My Head Is Amy Poehler,* **15**

AMY SHERMAN   *Get Me Off This Plane!,* **17**

VICTORIA SUN   *Silence,* **20**

KIM KIESEWETTER   *Teen Mom,* **22**

NYANKA J.   *Scratch and Sniff Feminist Choosing Invisibility,* **24**

CATHERINE CONANT   *The Bathmat,* **27**

COURTNEY BAKLIK   *Please Do Not Attempt to Enter When the Door Is Locked: A Guide to Pumping at Work,* **29**

ALENA DILLON   *If the Suit Fits,* **32**

ANNE BAGAMERY   *Clean Copy,* **34**

LEIGHANN LORD   *In Search of the Black Female Superhero,* **37**

LAURA ROSSI   *A Special Education,* **39**

MARIA DECOTIS   *My Zia,* **41**

JULIA MARRINAN   *Horse Girl,* **43**

NICOLE CATARINO   *Peanut Butter and Jelly,* **45**

SUZETTE MARTINEZ STANDRING   *Freak Paralysis,* **47**

EBONY MURPHY-ROOT   *Life Coach,* **50**

LESLIE MORGAN STEINER   *Women and Children First,* **53**

PAMELA KATZ   *Why Women Kill,* **56**

PATRICIA WYNN BROWN   *Butter Knives,* **59**

ANGELA AISEVBONAYE   *In Loving Reference to Ire,* **61**

AMY WHIPPLE   *Maybe-Visions,* **63**

RYAN WILTZIUS   *Whatever Happens Just Does,* **66**

CINDY EASTMAN   *Just Say YES,* **69**

LISA CHAU   *Walking the Tightrope,* **71**

ASHALIEGH CARRINGTON   *Black People Don't Do This,* **74**

DEBORAH HOCHMAN TURVEY   *Fierce Women of All Age,* **77**

HEIDI MASTROGIOVANNI   *Our Monikers,* **79**

NIAMH CUNNINGHAM   *What's in a [Last] Name?,* **81**

PEGGY TANNER   *Fierce Is In,* **83**

POLLY INGRAHAM   *State of My Soul,* **85**

LAURIE LAIDLAW   *May the Fierce Be with You,* **87**

NICOLE DECKER-LAWLER   *Speak Your Truth,* **89**

SHERRY PINAMONTI   *Battle of the Pregnancy Bulge,* **91**

HANNAH BALLOU   *A Poem to Miss Carriage on the
                                  Occasion of Lockdown,* **93**

LINDSEY KEEFE   *Bread and Rocks,* **96**

MEG SOMMERFELD   *Mom and the Night Visitors,* **98**

JENNIFER FORREST   *Breaking Out of the Blue Box,* **100**

RHEA HIRSHMAN   *I'm a Jewish Girl from Brooklyn, and
                                  My Story Is About Nuns,* **102**

MARISA ELANA JAMES   *The Refugees, the Rabbi, and the
                                  Times Square Police,* **105**

LISA SMITH MOLINARI   *The Sandwich Queen Manifesto,* **108**

EMILY PARROW   *Genealogy and the Anatomy
                                  of an Heirloom,* **110**

JENNIFER RIZZO   *I Broke Up with My Family Over Facebook,* **113**

EMILY TOTH   *The Night I Made Them Squirm,* **115**

JENNIFER SAGER   *Breathe,* **118**

DANIELLE WARING   *The Irrevocable Moments,* **120**

PAT MCGRATH   *How Radiation Helped Me Use My Voice,* **122**

NANCY BOCSKOR   *The Year of Living Cautiously
                        After a Life of Living Large,* **124**

LAURA CAPARROTTI   *Do Not Deal with a Woman Caparrotti,* **126**

JOAN SELIGER SIDNEY   *What a Life!,* **128**

BETH BLATT   *In Their Words,* **130**

LOUISA BALLHAUS   *Close,* **133**

MONA FRIEDLAND   *Perfectly Imperfect,* **135**

SUZY JOHNSON   *The Inheritance,* **137**

MARY ANN CAWS   *Rage Begins at Home,* **139**

PIA L. BERTUCCI   *Middle Sister,* **141**

JANE COOK   *Writing Saved Me,* **144**

GEORGIA COURT   *I May Be a Karen,* **147**

LIA LEVITT   *Knicks Chick,* **149**

FAITH PEASE   *A-L-C-O-H-O-L,* **151**

SALLY KOSLOW   *Plot Twist,* **153**

FIONA PITT-KETHLEY   *The So-What Factor,* **156**

JAMIE SPRIGGS   *Canoe,* **158**

TRACY STRAUSS   *The Bark Test,* **160**

MIRANDA WRIGHT   *Senior Project,* **162**

SHEREE R. MARCUCCI   *Second Acts, Or My Year of 50,* **164**

BONNIE JEAN FELDKAMP   *The Bridge Ladies,* **166**

BARBARA COOLEY   *Thin Ice,* **169**

YVONNE RANSEL   *Put a Smile on Your Face,* **171**

TERI RIZVI   *Living in the Moment,* **173**

CONTRIBUTORS   **175**

ABOUT THE EDITOR   **201**

Introduction

GINA BARRECA

Fierce can be getting out of bed. It can be taking a shower. It can be switching a job, seeing a shrink, going to war, or getting out of a relationship that could kill you. It can be crossing your arms across your chest or opening them in an embrace.

A fierce woman is fierce in belief, in joy, in compassion, in commitment, in intelligence, in wit, and in community. She's capable not only of finding her own way but of creating a path for others; she doesn't just break down doors, she tears down walls.

A fierce woman makes her deadlines, makes the call she dreads, makes good on her promises, and makes trouble when necessary—but only when necessary. She is not a coward: She accepts responsibility but won't carry somebody else's guilt—she's no sin-eater, no doormat, and no blotting pad silently soaking up whatever drops on her from above or seeps into her from the sides. She doesn't cry wolf until the wolf is at the door, or until she needs to call the rest of the pack to join her for significant and meaningful lupine backup.

A few of us were born fierce, but most of us had to learn it.

I was in high school when I started to find my own courage and overcome my sense of trepidation about life, but that sense of confidence and fearlessness came at a cost.

I grew up fast, and not on purpose. My mother—an immigrant and a shy, sad woman—was diagnosed with cancer when I was fifteen; I looked after her during her unendurable illness. She died during my junior year of high school. My father was a devoted parent, but he worked long days and couldn't look after the day-to-day life of a teenage girl.

There was nothing to do but look after myself. I learned to stop waiting for someone else to provide comfort, or solace, or apologies. I stopped depending on anyone—parent, family members, teachers, boyfriends, or friends—to define who I was or who I might become.

As I accepted the need to think about my future and map my own destiny, I also started thinking about ways that women—not only me but all women—had for too long permitted others to define our lives.

This ranged all the way from allowing the government to rule on our health care and reproductive freedom to the simple way we learned to doubt our own judgment in small matters. We were told that others knew better, that the world had always worked a certain way and some things couldn't change, that we'd learn to relax once we slid into conventional femininity.

I still hate being told to "relax." That, along with "Calm down already" and "Why are you making such a big deal about this?" are phrases that make me want to bear arms.

Being told to relax, not to think we're so special, not to bother ourselves with "things we don't understand" have been such effective weapons in the arsenal used to keep women circumscribed, it's easy to believe that it isn't worth the effort to revise or rebel against what's already been determined to be in our best interest.

Women are told, repeatedly and with authority, that we don't know what's best for us. The lingering effects of those early and destructive childhood lessons are that girls distrust our own instincts, insights, and wishes.

For thousands of years, every generation of women has made the road easier for other girls to follow. The women who paved the way for us did it through their own fearlessness, making sure that women got the vote, could use birth control, could legally terminate an unwanted pregnancy, could choose children or choose not to be a mother, could choose being single or life with a partner—and we've shown courage in maintaining and widening those choices for the young women facing their futures now.

Yet we're not done: Rights need to be defended even after they are won.

No one should curtail her ambitions, skills, or energy, or be defined by an outsider's version of herself—especially not because somebody thinks she's not up to the challenge.

The real discovery, as many of the pieces here illuminate, is the moment when we realize that slipping off conventional feminine propriety is like stripping out of a too-tight dress. And kicking off the Goody Two-shoes pretense is like sending a pair of high heels flying across the room after a long day. The big changes in women's lives do not necessarily involve menopause or the end of child-rearing or any other Margaret Mead anthropological slide show; the biggest thing that happens to any woman is when she stops being the ingenue—when she realizes that she can speak up, speak out, and make herself heard.

When I was young, divorced, and living on New York's Lafayette Street in a small, shabby, rent-stabilized apartment, the building's superintendent announced that everybody's windows were going to be replaced.

This information would not have been unwelcome—the old windows were made of creaky, swollen wood—except for one detail: The news was delivered during an arctic winter night, one of those tough years when Manhattan's tall buildings turn the streets into wind tunnels. It was bad window-replacing weather and could only have been the work of landlords who had just figured out they were losing money by losing heat.

Or maybe somebody smart actually explained to them how heat worked—whatever.

The impossibly bizarre idea of taking out and replacing all the windows in a three-floor apartment house during a series of snowstorms could only have been prompted by bad management and poor planning, as well as an almost farcical disregard for the tenants.

It didn't bother me that a bunch of guys were coming over to work in the apartment. I figured it would be fine—they'd do their job, and it would all be over soon. I made a big pot of coffee to show them some gratitude for their hard work.

Work hard they did: Four burly men removed the windows in a matter of minutes. The temperature in the apartment instantly dropped 30 degrees, and snow started settling on the sills as they readied the replacements. Huffing and grunting, they lifted the new windows into place.

There was one problem, however. The new windows didn't fit into the frames.

The new windows were the wrong size.

The old windows, broken into unusable pieces, lay in heaps in the poorly lit hallway outside my apartment door.

We all looked at one another, the guys and me. The wind howled.

"We'll put some plastic sheeting over the windows," the head guy explained. "We'll come back tomorrow."

Snow is blowing into my apartment. I live in a second-story apartment, all my windows are gone, and this guy says he'll put in plastic sheeting to get me through the night?

Not only would the place become a tundra within the hour; by dawn, sixteen homeless people would be living with me, having made their way through the gaps in the plastic sheeting to set up, with full squatter's rights, a new life on my fold-out couch.

That's when I started to yell.

Let's say I suggested that plastic sheeting over four windows would offer inadequate protection. I did not say it in those words.

There was silence.

Well, it wasn't really silent because the wind was picking up and some loose pieces of broken wood were banging against the empty window frames, as if signaling to the world that a single thirty-one-year-old was ready to receive all guests.

Four large men stood in front of me as I raved.

"HOW COULD YOU NOT MAKE SURE YOU HAD THE RIGHT WINDOWS BEFORE YOU KNOCKED OUT THE OLD ONES?"

I used those words—but added additional ones.

More silence.

The head guy paused before he finally met my eyes and barked, "You're not perfect either, lady."

That, friends, remains, in my experience, one of the most astonishing statements ever made to a disgruntled customer: "You're not perfect either, lady."

"Yeah, that's true," I agreed. "But I didn't just go to YOUR house, break YOUR windows, and then suggest you sleep under a couple of extra blankets until tomorrow."

I must have looked as fierce as I felt, because within two hours, they sent trucks to Queens, got new workmen from the Bronx, and installed perfectly fitted windows. The lessons here? You don't need to be perfect in order to insist that somebody treat you like a person; just because you try to offer someone a warm greeting, it doesn't mean they won't leave you out in the cold; learning how to raise hell is a useful and often underrated skill.

Fierce women will tell you the truth, and we won't sugarcoat it. We'll laugh only when your stories are funny; we'll argue until the sun goes down or comes up again without batting an eye—let alone fluttering an eyelash in a flirtatious attempt to get you to settle down.

We don't want to settle down anymore. We've been settled, like some western township, and now we want to kick up the dust and tear down the fences. Not only will we not settle down, we won't settle for less than what we've always wanted: a good time and a fair fight.

The seventy-five essays you're about to read offer windows into the lives of formidable, funny, and ferociously bold women.

Here's to a bright and fierce future.

Gina Barreca

Dying to Be Better

CAROLINE LEAVITT

It's pre-pandemic and I'm on the NYC subway and I'm dying. Not "dying from the heat" or "dying from the crowds of people stuffed into the car." I mean I am really and honestly dying, having come out of a three-and-a-half-week medical coma, a four-month hospital stay, and another six months recuperating at home from a rare, nearly always fatal blood disease I contracted after giving birth to my son. So why am I on the subway? Because my husband lost his job because "he was spending too much time caring for me and our baby." Because Suze, an old acquaintance of mine who works at Victoria's Secret, promised to give me a fashion catalog to write, which would pay for three months of our mortgage while I struggled to get better.

"Can you messenger it to me?" I had begged, and Suze had laughed. "Don't be silly. I want to see you. You always look so adorable."

That was the problem: her seeing me. When she had last seen me, it had been at Macy's, where we both worked, writing about fashion. Back then, I was lithe and skinny with a mop of long, dark curly hair and complicated earrings. I had Victorian pale skin and wine-red lipstick, and I wore tight little vintage jackets and short skirts to show off my legs, toned from ballet. But now? My entire body was bloated from toxic meds so that the only thing that fit me was a muumuu. I had a huge moon face, courtesy of prednisone. My hair had literally slid from my head months ago, so I had to wear a silk scarf over my balding head. My skin was no longer porcelain. Oh, no. It was gray. And not pretty dove gray. Old wet cardboard gray.

But we had no money, and I had to go.

When I got to the Victoria's Secret building, I was winded. But I had to do this.

I entered the office, all pink pearl colors and soft coral carpet. Of course every woman in the office was tall and thin and luscious-haired. They didn't walk. They glided. And when I told the woman at the desk I was there for Suze, she said, "Really?" punching down buttons in her phone.

Suze came out, sleek as a racehorse, her blonde hair swishing to her waist, and I watched her face, how it stalled as if it didn't know what expression to be. But she had a packet in her hand—my packet! My money I could earn! I drew myself up again. She came closer and I hated myself for apologizing, but I did. "I'm sorry I look like this," I murmured.

"Don't be silly!" she said. She glanced at the sweat on my muumuu, at the kerchief around my head, at my skin too. And then she drew herself up too, as if she were deciding something. "I'm so sorry you came all this way in," she said. "The project was canceled!"

Her smile was bright and hard as candy. "Good to see you," she said.

We both knew she was lying on both counts.

Outside again, I walked to calm myself. And then I passed one store and there was a bright green sleeveless minidress. I never wore green. Bright colors to me were like garlic to a vampire.

Plus, my bloated gray arms would show, and so would my legs. Worse, it was clingy fabric, and was my shape a shape anyone would want to see?

That dress called to me. It shouted and insisted. It wouldn't be ignored.

I walked into the store and tried that dress on. I stuffed the muumuu in a corner of the dressing room and then paid for the new dress I was wearing.

Outside, I felt cooler. I didn't walk. I strutted. To me, that new dress was hope. That dress was the future. Maybe that dress was my "fuck you" to anything or anyone who was going to tell me: You can't be who you are right now. Were people looking at me? When they did, my grin grew two sizes. If it was more than one person and they murmured something to another, I called out, "Beautiful day, right?" I made them see me. I made them respond.

I looked down at my new green dress. It was the color of a go signal. This dress was perfect.

It was alive. You know what else? So was I.

Secret Rites

PHILLIS LEVIN

On my bedroom's oak floor, when I was three, lay two oval rugs spaced several feet apart, the same intertwining flowers and leaves woven into them, the same pale fringe surrounding their borders. Those rugs became two islands: The ritual I devised involved sitting on one and, without standing up, moving to the other without touching the floor. From one island to the other, without falling into the water. In summer, when heat and humidity interrupted my sleep, I'd crawl out of bed and lie on the floor, resting my cheek on the blessedly cool wood surface, ignoring the rules about drowning.

• • •

When my parents took me shopping for clothes, I'd wander off sometimes. At some point I'd reach into a coat pocket or the seam of a garment to find a stray thread and take it out—careful not to snag the fabric, simply removing what no longer was necessary. Winter coats were especially good. I would hold the thread and, still concealed from view, place it in one of my own pockets or wrap it around a button on my blouse. Or I'd pull a stray thread from something I was wearing and place it in the pocket of a coat I admired; this way, I could be elsewhere, live inside that pocket wherever it would go. What thrilled the most was knowing someone might buy this coat, that the two of us would be joined, my thread carried by whoever wore that coat. Unrelated threads, connected. A remnant. Relic of the impossible. Would anyone reach into this pocket one day and discover a thread that didn't belong?

• • •

I am a child no longer. The first year of college, when a friendship starts in an instant, an affinity grasped at first sight, before a word is spoken: knowledge tangible as an electrical charge. Within a week we are talking every day; she reads my poems, sets some of them to music. One evening, as we sit across from each other in the campus pub, a candle between us on the table, the slowly burning flame suddenly goes out. I strike a match to reignite the candle, and we notice how the flame leaps from the matchhead to the wick, jumping an unexpected distance. That's when the experiment, which will become our daily ritual, begins: We take turns blowing out the candle, holding a lit match as far from the wick as possible to see how far the little flame can travel. Most marvelous is when the flame traces a circuitous path. A jolt of joy united us when the vapor trail was lit and a new flame leapt to the wick. In the future, on the rare occasion I demonstrate this phenomenon to anyone, it will be met with surprise.

The following spring, she decided to cut the thread between us, break the attachment, put out the candle. The sentence on our friendship was passed without warning or recourse. We lose touch. She is ahead of me by two years. Unexpectedly, she appears at my graduation ceremony; we embrace under a sheer blue sky, never see each other again. Later I hear she has enrolled in a seminary, has taken vows and is a nun. Recently, at the frayed end of a search trailing many tangled threads, I find a series of essays she has published and from a biographical note learn she is an Orthodox Christian monastic who trained in psychotherapy, Mother of a monastery dedicated to fostering recon-ciliation. Missing thread; thread of flame. Should I call her, write to her—or let the severed thread dangle?

• • •

My students laugh in one of our Zoom poetry workshops, a bit of relief during the pandemic. We've let our guard down, tell silly stories about things we did in childhood. I've encouraged them to recall visual memories. I confess my ritual of the two oval rugs—the agility required to avoid any part of my body touching the floor, a death by drowning. "The floor is lava!" one of them calls out from a square somewhere on my screen. I don't understand what they're talking about, why they can't stop laughing, until a student explains that "The Floor Is Lava" is a game they played as children, its rules akin to the rules I had established—except that the floor is molten rock instead of water.

• • •

These days, I touch the floor and do not drown.

• • •

Have you ever put your hand in your pocket and found a thread that doesn't belong?

As God Is My Witness

CHEYENNE SMITH

Dear Jehovah God

At a young age, you are made painfully aware that you're different from the other kids at school. The other kids don't have to spend their Mondays, Thursdays, and Sundays in a church that's not a church.

What's it called again?
It's a Kingdom Hall.

The other kids aren't dictated to sit still and listen to the preaching of men—always men. The elder brother stands in front of the podium in his crisp suit and tie. The brother illustrates the image of our Father. He, a perfect being, chose to love us, his flawed creations. We were born with sin embedded in us, and it is in our nature to commit acts of depravity. We are wicked people in a wicked world filled with wicked things. This is of our own doing, not the Father's. Yet as long as we worship and obey, we will receive His undeserved kindness and mercy. You listen as the brother makes promises and vows on your behalf. These are oaths that you are not even sure you understand. When the prayer ends, you are reminded that He is always watching.

Help me to maintain your image in the presence of my peers.

Years later and you are on the brink of pubescence. The jagged road to get there has not been easy. "Growing pangs" doesn't cover it. Little kids have yet to step into their roles as judge and jury. Any questions they have stem from curiosity.

How come you don't celebrate birthdays?
Why don't you pledge allegiance to the flag?

But then those little kids grow up, and those questions become condemnations.

She's one of the people who knocks on your door in the mornings.

Those judgments are heavy on your shoulders. Eventually, the weight is no longer something you can bear. And relief leads to your disgrace. It's a

Friday afternoon and you're sitting on the bus. The new Kanye West song crackles through the radio speakers. Every kid raps along word for word except you. Your mother would be horrified if she heard the filth spewing from his mouth. When it gets to Nicki Minaj's part, the energy is instantly electrified. Kids bob their heads and throw their hands up. Hidden underneath your bed sheets, you've listened to this song.

And now you just look at the camaraderie among your peers and for the hundredth time you want to join them. This time that desire spurs action. There is nothing more that you want than acceptance. When Nicki's words glide past your lips, you finally get it.

"Now look at what you just saw, this is what you live for,
I'm a muthafuckin monster."

The approval you receive almost distracts you from the guilt clawing at you. You hope that He is somehow not watching.

Help me to resist in the face of temptation.

In high school, you never go to parties. When you attend your first college party, it is a shock to your system.

Don't forget Him and everything that you've been taught.

You now understand why your mother didn't want you to leave home. Colorful lights flash and dubstep blares through the speakers. The girls grind into the groins of boys who greedily grasp at their hips. It's entirely claustrophobic, yet everyone seems so free. You feel out of place, but you don't look it. Your neon tube top and skin-tight jeans are a stark contrast to the frilly dresses you used to wear. You're overcome by how sexy and desirable you feel. You stare into a cup that had been handed to you.

What is it?

Vodka mixed with Sprite, maybe? Definitely vodka, though.

You bring the cup to your lips and sip debauchery. There's a small hope you're somehow hidden from His piercing gaze in this dingy basement.

Help me to be a good girl

The first time a boy touches you, you cry. It's a shock to both of you. The boy is freaking out.

Did I do something wrong?

If only he knew how much you wanted it, how good you were feeling. You have become what you were warned against. You are that unclean thing that He hates. You have become the condition to that unconditional love.

In Jesus's name

There are times where you will look in the mirror. You note the changes that you see.

Am I withering or blooming?

You can't help but wonder if He still watches you.

Amen.

How "Pretty Pretty Princess" Helped Me Find Love, aka Spin Your Way to Romance and Jewelry

LARA SCALZI MEEK

My favorite board game as a child was "Pretty Pretty Princess," the groundbreaking, revolutionary game for ages five to ninety-nine. To win the game and be crowned the Pretty Pretty Princess, you spin the dial in the center of the circular board and move your jeweled token around the spaces. You must collect all six pieces of plastic jewelry from your chosen color set—a bracelet, a necklace, a ring, two earrings, and the silver jeweled crown—to be victorious. Jewels sparkle in their box, calling out to the little girls around the board to be crowned and claim their glory.

Forget "Monopoly"; my friends and I didn't want to own the world. We wanted to rule it.

As I entered my teen years, "Pretty Pretty Princess" went with me. At seventeen, my girlfriends and I convinced my boyfriend at the time to play "Pretty Pretty Princess" with us. It took a bit of prodding, but he reluctantly agreed to play with us after several eye rolls and exasperated groans. Though after a few spins of the dial, it became obvious his heart wasn't in it. It made me wonder, who was this commoner among royalty? Why couldn't he put aside some misplaced masculine pride and have some silly fun with us—or at least try not to diminish the joy of others? He eventually lost the game, and my affection.

Later, a college boyfriend agreed to play with my girlfriends and me. He kept telling us that it was our idea, he was just doing it to make us happy, and that this was stupid, but it didn't take much prodding. Every time he put on an item of jewelry, he reminded us that he didn't want to do this, but it was the rules so he had to wear them.

After a few rounds, I began to think the gentleman doth protest too much. I noticed that he put the earring on straight, moved the necklaces to center, and correctly placed the ring with its gem upright. When he lost the game, he breathed a sigh of relief and said he didn't care anyway, but he took his time removing the jewelry.

A few months later when he asked to wear my lingerie, it didn't come as too much of a surprise. I may only play princess, but I have no problem with queens. I tried to talk to him about his sexuality, but he shut down and refused to talk. "Pretty Pretty Princess" had once again shown me the truth inside my current paramour. As national treasure and incomparable goddess RuPaul often says, "If you don't love yourself, how in the hell you gonna love somebody else?" I'm sure if my "Pretty Pretty Princess" could talk, it would have also spelled out "mother issues" with the little plastic jewelry pieces.

One year later, during my last summer at home, "Pretty Pretty Princess" found its way back in the spotlight. I was looking through old board games with my friends and upon finding my dear "Pretty Pretty Princess," I demanded we play.

The guy with us agreed without hesitation. To say he wanted to win would be an understatement. He wanted to destroy us.

He adorned himself with every piece of jewelry, adding a flourish and dramatic eye-bat. He informed my friend that the blue of his jewelry brought out the color of his eyes, while the yellow hue of her jewelry was washed out by her complexion. Though psychological warfare was not mentioned in the rules, he understood it was implied.

When he made his final spin of the dial—with his bejeweled hand, he moved his token gracefully—he landed on the crown. His coronation was brief, but filled with ridicule for his fellow players. My friend was shocked, crying out, "I can't believe you beat us!" As he gracefully removed his adornments he looked at us and said, "Of course I beat you. I always play to win." Here, at last, "Pretty Pretty Princess" had found me a man who would throw himself 100 percent into whatever he did. He would joyfully follow where I lead, but never stop being true to himself.

Five years later, he asked me to marry him and then let me loose in a jewelry store to pick out a ring so I'd have exactly what I wanted. After all, you can't expect a man to treat you like a princess unless he knows what it feels like to be one.

Fierce Skin

MAUREEN CORRIGAN

"Fierce" is not a word that resonates with me. When I was growing up in 1960s Queens, women weren't called "fierce." They were called "tough," "not nice," "a 'B,'" or "that-one-sure-has-a-mouth-on-her." These were the kinds of women who stood outside their apartment houses on summer nights gossiping and giving anyone who walked by direct stares. These women didn't bother to "fix themselves up" to do their grocery shopping; they wore housedresses, and God help you if you banged into their shopping cart in the narrow aisles of the local Key Food.

"Fierce" in that time and place meant "mean," and I was scared of "fierce." My mother certainly wasn't fierce; she was gentle, childlike even, and so shy that she would sometimes ask the teenage me to speak for her when she needed to return something at a store. She was always ashamed of her lack of education; during the Depression, she'd had to leave high school after one year to work at a factory. I too was shy, but I had better grammar, so I was her public mouthpiece. Otherwise, if you ask anyone who knew me from kindergarten through graduate school what I was like, I guarantee the first thing they'll say is "She was quiet."

But there was one thing about me that *was* fierce: my skin.

In sixth grade, my skin began breaking out and kept raging for years. When I say, "breaking out," I don't mean a discreet blemish here or there; I mean red, angry, pimples—the kind that were called "carbuncles." I have scars on my face from these pimples. I do not wear them proudly.

I see very few young people anymore with this kind of acne. But back then, the dermatologist my parents sent me to only had tetracycline and sunlamps in his arsenal. The sunlamps made my skin peel so that for days, I'd have a face full of dead skin flakes on top of my pimples. One Saturday, I showed up to my regular appointment and was greeted by a substitute doctor. "You have dandruff of the face!" he joked. (What kind of creep says that to a teenage girl?) Neighborhood experts also weighed in on my appearance: "You're a pretty girl," a pharmacist once told me when I went to pick up my tetracycline. "But you need to drink more water." (Doesn't everybody?) The "fierce" women simply stared.

After a year, the dermatologist changed receptionists. The new receptionist was—I kid you not—one of the most beautiful girls at my high school. She was Italian, with glossy black hair and alabaster skin. Every other week I'd stand before her with my inflamed, peeling skin, writing out a check for my treatment. She'd gaze at me with the cool direct look of those fierce women.

Repressed memories of this era erupt like . . . well, I won't finish the metaphor. There was the time when I applied for a part-time job at Macy's on 34th Street in Manhattan. The woman who interviewed me (not fierce, but firm) told me my complexion was too bad to work on the floor, but if I came back in two weeks and my skin was better, I might be hired. I drank water for two weeks and lived on plain rolls with ricotta cheese. (Bland food was another folkloric cure for acne.) Mind over matter works for short periods, so my skin did get a little better and I got the job at Macy's, working the cash register in the dim corner of the "Husky Boys" department. My chubby customers and I recognized each other for what we were: exiles from those better departments designed for those closer to the desired ideals of beauty.

Decades away from that torment, I sometimes mull over the empowering notion that my angry skin might have been "speaking" for my shy young self.

Maybe my pimples were yelling too. Maybe they were shouting to those fierce women: "Stop looking at me. I don't want to be like you." Maybe they were singing to the boys I was nervously attracted to in high school: "Keep your distance! I don't need any complications!" Maybe, in chorus, they were singing, real loud: "The life of the mind is more sustaining than temporary youthful beauty!"

I wasn't fierce back then, but my skin was. I'm tougher now.

One thing I know: Once you've lived with pimples as a teenage girl, the wrinkles of age can't scare you.

Niloufar Comes to America

NILOUFAR REZAI

Come into my eyes, and look at me through them,
for I have chosen a home far beyond what eyes can see.
—Rumi

Niloufar-eh-Abi, Blue Morning Glory: My father's tailor shop in Tehran was named after me, his only daughter. I felt regal that my name adorned a storefront awning. It was conveniently located near the hospital where my mother was a nurse.

Picture a crisp autumn morning in Tehran in 1971, and imagine my parents as they begin their workday: My father opens his shop and my mother continues walking to the hospital where she, a nurse, has to clear security—a novel event in an otherwise safe city.

She knew work would be a little different on this day. Surrounded by SAVAK (the intelligence organization of Iran) and by a multitude of foreign surgeons (in this scenario, "foreign" refers to American), my mother enters the operating room and scrubs into what will become a life-changing series of events.

Tadj ol-Malouk, or Malekeh, a seventy-five-year-old female patient, is undergoing, by today's standards, a routine operation: cataract surgery. During this period in history, however, cataract removal was a complicated and involved procedure requiring a hospital stay with a significant recovery period. Ensuring that world-class surgeons perform this surgery is a luxury afforded to those like Malekeh, otherwise known as Her Royal Highness.

And soon, me, the daughter of a tailor and a nurse.

My mother handed over scalpels, suctions, and scissors on demand to the team of six surgeons as they proceeded to remove the cataracts of the Queen of Iran, mother to Mohammad Reza Shah Pahlavi. A conversation ensued between the four American eye surgeons from New York City and their Iranian colleagues. "Our nurse, Mrs. Rezai, has a small child born with eye issues," noted Dr. Jamshidi. *"Khonoomeh Rezai, begooh behesh rejebeh dokhtaret."* ("Mrs. Rezai, tell him about your daughter"). My somewhat timid mother, through her surgical mask, whispered in Farsi, *"Aghah Doktohr, khahesh meekonam, shohmah?"* ("Mister Doctor, please will you?")

While extracting a royal cataract, the head surgeon, Dr. Ken Galin, who had been listening carefully, insisted, "Bring us the child." The team was scheduled to remain in Tehran for only a short time, so I was expeditiously scheduled to be evaluated. Within a day, I lay on an operating table with a team of surgeons fit for a queen standing over me.

Hours of surgery passed, and I was sent to recover on a dedicated floor of the hospital where the only other patient was the Queen Mother. After several days of lying in a hospital bed with sandbags to keep my head still post-surgery, my parents were informed of my prognosis:

"We have to monitor your daughter closely. She will likely need additional procedures to ensure her vision is fully restored. You will have to travel to America regularly for follow-up appointments." So pronounced Dr. Galin.

"My name is Niloufar," I announced to my kindergarten teacher, smiling, proud, wearing pigtails and sporting Coke-bottle glasses. She countered, and I accepted, "We'll call you Jennifer."

It wasn't until the school-scheduled parent-teacher conference that my mother became aware of the new name I'd been summarily assigned. She thought perhaps she'd entered the wrong classroom—who was this "Jennifer" to whom the teacher kept referring? It took her a moment, but then my mother, in her newly-acquired English, denounced the false name in favor of the Persian one she and my father had thoughtfully assigned. "She name for flover," my mother annunciated. "Vaht mean dat name? Vaht Jen . . . jenfur?"

It was 1976, only three short years after leaving our homeland, that my mother, Roza, also named for a flower, found herself in this seemingly ridiculous argument. She wondered if my teacher knew, despite her accent and uncertain English elocution, that she was an intelligent, fierce, and educated woman who had sacrificed her career, home, and family for her child. She was amazed by the audacity that someone would change another person's name to simplify their own existence.

Yes, some nods had been made toward simplicity: *Niloufar-eh Abi* was replaced by "Nilo Cleaners." It became well known in Manhattan and was located a few short blocks from the eye specialists we moved to be near.

With no English, little money, and even less hesitation, my parents set out for what was to be a temporary stay in "Amreeca": Fifteen eye surgeries, a revolution, and forty-eight years later, we remain.

● ● ●

The Soul is a stranger trying to find a Home
somewhere that is not a where.
—Rumi

It is fortunate that I inherited my mother's fierceness. Both my son and daughter were born with congenital cataracts. At two weeks old, they each had surgery—and it was performed by the former medical student who accompanied the surgical team in Iran.

The Voice Inside My Head Is Amy Poehler

MIA YANOSY

I'm sitting on my bed in my first dorm room, which is at a Catholic college. A friar has just knocked on my door to bless our room with holy water. Our entire building—ten floors—is girls only, so the mere sight of a man is a surprise.

Later, I hate when people say that religion isn't pervasive at Catholic colleges. There's a friar in my dorm room.

My roommate isn't here. Usually I prefer it that way, because I have no patience with her. She is good-hearted, but I am miserable and can't take even normal friend behavior. Everything gets heated in my mind. When she brags about getting an A on a paper, I hate her. When she says the Connecticut license plate is ugly, I hate her. When we argue about what is the correct word for a water fountain, I hate her. We spent the first few weeks of school eating most meals together, and now I hide from her in the dining hall. Still, it would be nice to not be alone with the friar.

Thankfully, he has other rooms to bless. When he leaves I go back to what I was doing: staring at the poster on my wall. I can't for the life of me remember where I got it from or why I picked it out. It's the color of the sky on a sunny day and reads, "Great people do things before they're ready. They do things before they know they can do it." Apparently Amy Poehler said it. I think about this quote all the time because I was not ready to leave home, and now I'm in an anxious-depressive episode. I don't actually know that it's called "anxious-depressive" until years later. All I know now is that I feel full of holes.

I keep thinking about it as I listen to the friar make his way around the hall. Maybe it's not that great people *do* things before they're ready, but that they can in the first place. Maybe some people really can't do things before they know they can.

So now I hate my roommate and I hate Amy Poehler. She wrote a definition of greatness and I willingly taped it up to my wall, so I guess I have to believe in it. I don't know why I do that—trust Amy Poehler. I don't know a thing about her, other than that she's supposed to be funny. But what if she's right?

* * *

It's Saturday afternoon in late September, and I can't believe how badly I am failing. From my dorm window I can see down to the grass where everyone likes to lay their blankets and sunbathe. There are lots of kids there now, stretched out, books spread open. Sunbathing days are dwindling. I think I should be out there with everyone, but I don't want to be. That's the worst part of it all.

I don't want to leave to get lunch either, so I sit down at my desk to read for Civ. There is a pencil case on the shelf that breaks my heart. This is my life; pencil cases make me cry, and I can't tell anyone because I am the only one who knows what the pencil case really means. Later, when I think of this, I think of blackberries.

I can't read the *Iliad* because I'm arguing with Amy Poehler in my head. Who made her the expert on greatness anyway? I'll be great without her. I'll be greater *than* her. I'll be greater than the greatest person on this earth, and then I'll drown them, and Amy Poehler, in dirt with my great hands.

I should have asked the friar how he defines greatness. The whole point of religion is to answer the big questions, right? But it wouldn't matter; nothing he would say will make me feel better. Sometimes the only thing I really want is for Amy Poehler to show up at my dorm room and take back what she said. She could sit on the bed and tell me that someone made up that quote and attributed it to her. That way the poster would be wrong. Later, I move back to Connecticut, lose the poster. I go to a new school with lots of atheists.

Get Me Off This Plane!

AMY SHERMAN

The turbo fans crescendoed, nudging the DC-10 jet onto the runway. I was an American Airlines flight attendant on the last leg of a three-day trip, heading home to Chicago from Dallas.

Picking up speed, the engines suddenly went into reverse with a fury. I was pressed into my jump seat. The engines roared, struggling to stop the behemoth. We settled into a slow taxi and turned off the runway.

"Ladies and gentlemen, apparently there was a miscommunication in the tower, and we just avoided colliding with another aircraft that was landing perpendicular to our runway," the captain says over the PA. "I apologize for any concerns, but everyone is safe. Unfortunately, in the process of stopping so rapidly, we did blow two tires. And since there are no available gates, we're going to pull over to the tarmac, get them changed out, and be on our way."

An aborted takeoff is rare . . . a first for me.

Dallas was hot. We hooked up to an APU (auxiliary power unit) to avoid sweltering in the cabin. What the captain failed to realize was that we were about to be held hostage for three hours while maintenance found spare tires, removed what was left of the duds, and replaced them. Longer than our actual flight time to Chicago. It wasn't pleasant, but most of the 268 passengers made do, happy to be alive.

In my section, however, a man seated on the aisle was not happy. He was downright surly. He bullied me every chance he could.

"This is ridiculous," he pouted. "I can *not* just sit here. Get me off this plane."

"I'm so sorry, sir, but there are no gates open for us to return to. And maintenance is working as fast as they can to replace the tires."

"Well, it's taking forever. I'm done with American."

Lord, I hope so.

He was relentless. The other passengers silently observed as he wore me down. After too many ugly encounters, I went to the galley to cry. I didn't know how to deal with him.

I was the face of the company. I did what I could to make people comfortable. But I didn't have anything to do with the control tower, or maintenance. I could not rappel down to the ground and yell at the team working in 100-degree heat on fire-hot tires that exploded from friction while saving our damn lives. All 267 other passengers were acting like adults. It *was* a ridiculous situation I did NOT create.

I dried my eyes and grabbed a wooden hanger from a closet, in case there was a mutiny. I held it with both hands. It's a narrow, curved piece of hard wood I can tap in one palm. It just felt good.

Mr. Special would not stop. He accosted me at every passing. I went up to the cockpit to speak with the captain.

"There is a guy insisting he needs to get off the plane. He keeps hounding me. What can we do?"

"He seriously wants off?"

"Oh, he's serious. He's being a total jerk."

"Okay then. I'll arrange it. We'll get some truck stairs over here and get him off."

"OMG. Thank you!"

I trekked back to my section in the rear of my favorite aircraft.

"Sir, I need you to gather all your belongings; I've arranged for you to get off the plane."

"Wait. What?"

"Please get all your things; the captain is getting stairs to remove you from the plane."

"But . . . what will happen after that? How will I get another flight?"

"You'll have to make arrangements with an agent. You wanted off. Please get your things."

Nobody says a word. I did not back down. This man has made my life miserable for two hours. I was giving him exactly what he had asked for. He needed to get the hell up.

He followed me up to the front—out of section C, through section B, past First Class, to the door. I left him there to be met by a mobile stairway. He was somebody else's nightmare now.

I walked back to my section, feeling like I had just taken out the trash. When I got to section C, the entire cabin burst into applause and cheers.

They hated him as much as I did! My smile grew with joyous validation. I had never felt so powerful. I did love the job, but I needed to go home and get my ass off that plane.

Silence

VICTORIA SUN

In my family, we speak three languages: Cantonese at home, English at work, and silence as a family. We don't say sorry. We leave a peeled orange on their desk. We don't say I love you. We send cat videos with an emoji.

I've studied nine different languages. It is possible for me to argue for hours why contrary to popular opinion the syntax of American Sign Language is not similar to Chinese, or why French is an overall shitty language. In each language, there are words and phrases that don't translate well into English.

There is no word for brother or sister in Cantonese, only younger brother/sister or older brother/sister. Titles are entwined branches on our family tree. 婆婆 roughly translates to "mother's mother," which looks and sounds nothing like the character for "mom." The language gets more complicated when it comes to extended family. 舅母 is how you refer to your mother's brother's wife. To this day, I don't know the names of anyone outside of my immediate family. But I do know their titles, which is to say, I see you and I recognize what you mean to me.

How you read Chinese characters depends on context. My household of four dwindled as, one by one, my siblings and I went off to college. In Cantonese, we have a saying ". . . to death." We use it to mean you're doing something to excess. My mother would use this saying in situations ranging from my playing video games for too long to overworking myself. On Tuesdays, my mother sees me sit on Zoom for seven hours. She refrains from commenting on the clear exhaustion on my face or fifteen-minute intervals of screaming, but whenever I go down to the kitchen, there is an orange waiting for me on a plate.

Yesterday my mother said to me, "You know tomorrow is 外公's birthday." And I asked her who that was. She replied, "That's my father." In my twenty-one years on this planet, I had never heard her use the word for her father.

Yet I remember when the shelf we used for my grandfather's memory fell. My mother wordlessly got out the broom and swept away the ashes and continued to serve dinner. It would be a few years before we replaced his picture frame.

When my grandmother died, my mother was too busy raising three kids to attend the ceremony. My sister and I gathered around our laptop and watched as my brother, who was still in college, explained her Alzheimer's while my mother stood quietly in the other room. After the call was over, I hugged my mom and told her I love her in my American way. I had seen *Cinderella* and *Aladdin* on DVD. Did this make her an orphan too?

In high school, a girl in my class bravely performed her slam piece, "I Think My Mom Is Depressed," for our coffeehouse. I saw her mother's face after the show. I don't know if there is a word in Cantonese for depression.

The only time I've ever seen my mother cry is when we went back to China and visited her parents' burial ground. I was fourteen. We were there for two weeks, and it has been the closest I've ever come to fluency. It wasn't until years later when I was listening to a YouTuber that I realized it was tradition to make a scene when a loved one passed: the crying, and hysterics. It was almost comical when my mother's friends proceeded to light a firecracker and told me to run. When we all then raced down the large barren hill, I thought about the contrast of silent American cemeteries filled with grass and flowers to the noise, dust, and dirt where we now stood. After catching my breath, I asked why we were doing what we did. This is what they explained to me: "We must let the dead know we are here."

When they lit the incense as we later walked through the shrines, I was still distracted by trying to translate instructions in my head, only realizing after it happened that the ash had landed on my hand. The back of my hand stung as I bowed over twenty times in various spots in and around the shrine. Not saying a word, my mother held my hand, her thumb rubbing the mark.

Silence had always been the loudest language in my house.

Teen Mom

KIM KIESEWETTER

My parents recently sent me a photo I had never seen of freshly-seventeen me and my freshly born daughter (who surely was never so tiny!). The sweet photo of a mom and a newborn hit me in an unexpectedly weird and painful way. I kept staring at it on and off for hours. It was like looking at a stranger.

Was this me?

I started to cry.

I've only just been able to acknowledge that I remember very little from this time in my life. Not because I wasn't there—I most definitely was—but because the whole experience was traumatic.

I got pregnant the first time I had sex. He and I had a tumultuous relationship; he would die just a little over a year after this photo was taken. My daughter and I received no help from him—financially or otherwise.

After I got pregnant, my parents were shunned by people from our church. Barely able to fit in a desk at my high school as my belly swelled, I was called a "slut" and a "whore" by most of my peer group. Teachers awkwardly hid me away in the back corner of the classroom and suggested I wear baggier clothes to camouflage my shape. Even though I was a dorky school-lover and high achiever, because nobody at my school offered support, I chose to get an adult equivalency diploma.

Daily, or almost daily, panic attacks began to overwhelm me, but since I knew so little about pregnancy, I thought they were pregnancy symptoms.

After I gave birth at 10:30 in the evening with my parents in attendance, I was startled to find myself after everyone left . . . entirely alone. It was the most alone I had ever felt.

And while I would feel that loneliness for years to come, I would use it to fuel the rage of success I had in the aftermath of that experience. I wanted out from under the stigma. I wanted my daughter to never feel the way I did.

I left. I went. I did.

I've never had an abortion. I don't know what it is like. I would never dis-count the many ways we are shaped as humans, but "choosing life" doesn't eliminate the potential for trauma. Parenting can be trauma. Adoption can be trauma. I was deeply and permanently affected by being a teen mom. My parents were impacted. My sister. My daughter. Irrevocably and permanently.

My story turned out epically well for a teen mom. I went to college and grad school, and have been able to have, in my life, creative and rewarding work.

But I realize now that the adults in my life when I was a teen essentially offered me no alternative to "choosing life"; they insisted that adoption or parenting were the only way to avoid the trauma of abortion.

No one told me I could develop trauma responses from going through teen parenthood. (And real talk: I had a pretty good teen mom story by com-parison to some I know!)

No one told me that once I "chose life," I would be berated, shamed, and stereotyped for needing help to make it work. I understood why abortion WOULD be appealing; strangers and friends alike said horrific and hateful things to me, even as I proved myself to be a loving parent to my child

I thought I deserved it for "sinning."

You know who helped me when I was a single teen mom? The govern-ment. I received welfare payments (a whopping $250/month!) and food stamps. I had Medicaid. I got federal and state financial aid for college. Those practical supports are one of the major reasons I was able to better my life and become financially independent.

So I share all this to say, humbly, to my one-issue voter friends: If you are REALLY pro-life, go help the young single mom, not with pity, but with respect and compassion. Vote for strong social welfare programs so that vulnerable parents have the resources they need in order to be good parents with ade-quate supports. Banning/restricting abortion means more vulnerable people having babies—people who deserve the help to make it work.

Remember that there is no guaranteed escape from trauma when making *any* decision around an unexpected pregnancy. What a woman needs is honest, nonjudgmental support and the recognition that whatever she does will affect her life in ways that can never be predicted.

Whoever oppresses the poor shows contempt for their Maker . . .
—Proverbs 14:31

Scratch and Sniff Feminist Choosing Invisibility

NYANKA J.

I am invisible to the train conductor, the barista too. I revel in my invisibility; there's power in choosing it. I enjoy not having to smile or hyper-focus on not coming off as flirty when attempting to be a polite fucking human being. Invisibility is an underrated freedom.

Invisible me watches the old lady on the train. Being able to watch others freely is another perk of invisibility. She has a tattoo on her right calf. I want to bend over to scratch and sniff it. The scent would tell me everything about her life. I shape my mouth to ask her how long it's been since her last tattoo and if she has a tramp stamp too. I wonder if it was called a tramp stamp then. I say neither. The tattoo talks to me and tells me she is a feminist. I can tell by her scent.

Feminists smell like coffee and champagne. I know because, even invisible, it is how I smell too.

I crawl off the train, a demoness in casual work wear. Head held high emitting pheromones of don't-fuck-with-me.

Midtown Manhattan is a cesspool of dead dreams, dreamers, and the lost. My pheromones sometimes get lost in the cesspool's scent. On occasion, there is the random man who sees through my invisibility. It is never used for kindness.

I weave through the crowds of Herald Square. I am an expert at slithering through bodies. Sometimes I forget that I am a person walking through other people who have traumas, dramas, and whose lives might be epic tales waiting to be cracked open and consumed. If I focus on their stories, I may be late for work.

I balance on the edge of the sidewalk with the other experts at slithering through bodies; we know instinctively when the light will turn so we do not have to look to see. I step out onto the street bopping my head aggressively to the latest R&B. I am jerked out of my rhythm of instinct and invisibility by a pair of calloused hands.

I know I am still invisible because all the other people keep walking. I look down at my elbow, only to realize I have been grabbed by a stranger on his bike. Men have a way of ruining your rhythm.

He grins as if we are old friends. I tell him to fuck off. He ignores me the way he should've ignored me from the beginning. I release more phero- mones to ward off the weirdos and pray that this time it works.

● ● ●

Today I have decided I do not want to be invisible. I layer on makeup. Slide primer across my skin and pack on foundation. I slide the bright red lipstick across my plump lips; emerge from my house a beacon.

The train conductor smiles at me today. He flirts. I smile back, pretending to have never seen his eyes glaze over me daily for months. My invisibility then was a choice . . . right?

I know I am more beautiful than usual. I can tell by the eyes that linger on me longer than they ever would. The eyes and kindness are overwhelm- ing and uncomfortable. I remember why I prefer being invisible. Men have a way of ruining things we do for ourselves.

My newfound visibility opens doors, literally. I have noticed a 50 percent increase in door holding rates from strangers, both men and women. I've also noticed a 100 percent increase in smile rate to door holding. Even serv- ing me seems like their pleasure.

The thought makes me think twice. Am I shallow for using my visibility like this? I throw the thought down a deep well and smile at the police officer. His grin spreads across his face like butter in a hot cast-iron skillet. It stays there for longer than necessary. I turn away and prepare to slither through the crowds again.

Only I don't have to. The crowd parts and I glide, seductively and drunk off my visibility. It is so much better to be seen by choice. But I am visible to undesirable purveyors too. I sense them standing too close and looking too long at places that are not my face. I return the favor with a cold stare. Most of them look away ashamed.

I wonder if they are ashamed because my stare strips them uncomfortably naked; tells them that I am equal. Sometimes I think they know it is because I am choosing to be perceived, and that terrifies them.

The Bathmat

CATHERINE CONANT

There once was a time when a person could wander into a large department store and spend hours trying on clothing without any intention to buy, checking clearance racks for bargains and sampling expensive perfumes, all without feeling like it was actually a Date with Death.

It was on such a trip that, as I passed the Linens department with its perfectly folded towels and mountains of fluffy pillows, it occurred to me that I was overdue for a new bathmat. My current one was a Sponge Bob Squarepants beach towel some kid had abandoned in my yard, but I enjoyed a sense of justice dripping on his square face before kicking him to the corner.

Picking out a bathmat shouldn't be that difficult, but it was. Colors! Shapes! Sizes! Textures! All I wanted was something that would spare me from slipping on a wet floor and breaking a hip. I grabbed one and headed to the checkout where, to my surprise, the clerk wasn't a pleasant woman wearing a cardigan but a young man whose mother was most assuredly picking him up after work. It was like seeing an ostrich at a funeral.

I was almost to the counter when I was pushed aside by a young woman with two young men who slapped a giant Bed-in-a-Bag on the counter and announced, "We want a full cash refund for this."

Stunned, the young man gulped and asked to see their receipt. The woman said, "We don't need a receipt; just give us the cash."

He looked stricken, but politely explained that because they lacked a receipt, he could only give them a store credit and, pointing to a heap of the very same Bed-in-a-Bag on sale at 50 percent off, that the credit would only be half the original price. The woman leaned forward and snarled, "No, you're wrong; you're going to give me the full price, cash . . . now." As I watched, both men quietly moved to the sides of the counter so they were each no more than an arm's length from the boy.

Clearly this situation hadn't be covered in training. The kid phoned for his floor manager, then the upstairs office, frantically seeking any grown-up who knew what to do; but he was on his own, trapped in Retail Hell.

I considered the bathmat I was holding and decided I'd keep using the towel. But as I turned away, I heard the woman sneer, "Either you give me the cash right now or I'll go upstairs and tell them you called me a fucking bitch."

It was like watching a bunny being hunted by wolves. I could not leave that child there, alone. My mind went blank. I may have thought I was auditioning for a Clint Eastwood movie, or it was staged and a guy with a camera was about to leap out from behind the mattress pads. Regardless, I reached into my pocket, found a card, and stepped between the woman and the boy. I handed him the card and, speaking directly to him, said, "Excuse me; I am an attorney and I've heard this entire conversation. If you'd like, I'm happy to go to upstairs and tell them exactly what happened."

The woman growled in my ear, "Shut up, you stupid bitch."

OK, now it was personal.

Not taking my eyes off him I said, "Furthermore, if you'd like, I'll be happy to file a Vacca Stulta* lawsuit against this woman on your behalf and represent you pro bono!"

When I turned around, they were gone.

Stunned, we both exhaled and looked at each other. Tears slid down his face; he looked so very young. I said, "You're safe; you did all the right things." Even then it was not proper to hug a clerk in the Linens department.

"You're an attorney?" he asked.

"Nope, I'm a storyteller. I thought we needed a different story. Could I please have my card back?"

He looked down at his hand. "This is a customer card from Doogie's Dog House!"

"Yeah, I buy one more hot dog, I get one free."

He gave it back, we shook hands, and I left the bathmat on the counter. As I rode down the escalator I thought, *No, I am not an attorney; I am one goddamn tough old lady.*

• • •

*Vacca Stulta, Latin, "you stupid cow"

Please Do Not Attempt to Enter When the Door Is Locked: A Guide to Pumping at Work

COURTNEY BAKLIK

You're seated in a room with blank, white-washed brick walls—no windows. You're shackled to a faded black office chair by clear plastic tubes running from your chest and over your arms. There is a *drip, dripping* into sterile, measurement-marked bottles and a *whoosh, whooshing* insistently sucking at you.

Are you in a torture chamber? An S&M fantasy scene? Or are you lovingly engaged in an intimate task?

This guide is for anyone unfamiliar with the joys of pumping breast milk at work. If you are considering this pursuit, follow the following steps to success.

Step 1: Inform Your Coworkers

First, approach your boss (a genteel man in his sixties who, you will come to find, is visibly uncomfortable discussing "women's issues") for a conversation about the expulsion of your bodily fluids.

This communication will initially involve a series of euphemisms. For example, you may start with discreet emails apologizing for needing "mama time" during meetings. But later, around the time your second baby arrives and you're out of the neurons it takes to think up any more dainty expressions, simply yell down the hallway: "Pumping! Be there in a minute!"

Step 2: Get the Gear

How are your one-handed typing skills? You may want to invest in a refresher course, as keeping pumps on your breasts is not as simple as it sounds.

Alternately, you could procure yet another specifically-made, uncomfortable, expensive, cumbersome bra (multiply by five if you change your bra daily). Or, if you've $500 to spare, purchase pumps that fit inside your bra and, as a bonus, increase your cleavage four sizes (meaning you'll still need those extra bras).

Step 3: Make the Time

You have extra time in your workday, right?

You should pump every time your baby would nurse and more often if you pump fewer ounces than your baby would consume in a feeding, which is typical. (*Note*: You should send excited, emoji-filled texts to your partner, including pictures of milk-filled bottles, any time you get more than four ounces in a session.) This likely means you will need to pump at least twice each workday; a pump session may take twenty to thirty minutes.

How is your tolerance for flu-like symptoms? If you can wait an extra hour or two beyond when you would normally feed your baby, you won't need to schedule an additional break with your boss or beg an already-beset colleague to cover your duties. You could get mastitis from waiting this long, but a round of antibiotics should clear that up in a few days (disclaimer: antibiotics are not recommended for infants).

Step 4: Find a Secluded Location

Does one of these exist in your place of work? If you do manage to find this mystical private room, it will be located in the very furthest corner of the building from your office and will not get a Wi-Fi signal.

Those of you who prefer to be productive at work would be best served finding a way to pump in your own workspace. Try the options below.

- Cover the Windows and Lock the Door. You will now discover how many people have a key to your room. Be prepared to scramble to cover up, desperately shout at whoever is entering to "Please, wait!" and abandon the idea of upholding your personal dignity in your place of work. You should also be prepared for the embarrassment that comes with discovering that one of your nipples has not been securely stowed while talking to your boss following one of these instances.

- Tape an Unsightly but Unmissable Neon Orange Sign over the Door Handle. As you will come to see, a locked door is rarely a deterrent to entering a room. Even when your sign says, in all caps, "PLEASE DO NOT ATTEMPT TO ENTER WHEN THE DOOR IS LOCKED," you will be frequently entertained by repeated "jiggling" of your door handle, knocking on your door, intentionally loud complaining, and grumbling questions (*I really need my stuff! What are they doing in there?*). Hopefully the resulting anxiety won't affect your milk output (spoiler: it will).

A Final Note

All joking aside, if you come away from your pumping experience with most of your self-respect intact, consider the job well done. But even if you do lose a little along the way, allow yourself some applause for accomplishing this great feat in spite of the obstacles.

And maybe, because of you, your daughters won't have to face as many.

If the Suit Fits

ALENA DILLON

I remember being impressed by the heft of my wedding dress—ten pounds of delicious cream satin and tulle, every ounce vital to the resplendent sail designed to propel my partnership toward sunset. It took an entire decade before I was again struck by the sheer quantity of material dedicated to a single garment. This time, though, it wasn't a fairy-tale gown. It was a bathing suit.

By then, threads of wrinkles had branched from my once dewy eyes. My breasts had swelled, a transient perk, and then deflated and sagged. So had my belly. Once a young hopeful bride, now I was a mother, with all the doughy trappings I thought best wrapped up and kept out of sight, even at the beach—maybe especially at the beach. I was beginning to think the term "mother*hood*" came from the temptation to conceal oneself into obscurity.

The extent of the postpartum bathing suit shouldn't have surprised me. Hadn't *I* specifically searched for a one-piece tarp complete with tummy control and boy shorts? Hadn't *I* scrolled through and nixed offerings with a deep V-neck or arbitrary cutouts? Hadn't *I* requested overnight delivery? (If only childbirth delivery could have been so cheap.)

Yet, as my biceps strained to shimmy the garment from its plastic shipping sheath, and as the fabric cascaded down as a nylon-spandex blend waterfall, I experienced not the awe and reverence I had at the bulk of my wedding dress, but rather a distinct sense of dread.

I once wore white—or at least ivory. Now I bought black, which was fitting (as was my size large), because this was a mild sort of bereavement. I was mourning a self that was no longer (black, too, because it's slimming).

Beneath the dust of decades and stretch-mark squiggles, there was a maiden who'd honeymooned on black sand beaches in a string bikini, the slices of her top stretched lackadaisically over breasts that didn't need support because they mostly stayed in place on their own, the triangle bottom cutting aggressively up her supple rear. She was in her early twenties and knew of cellulose and white hair only as parables, a harbinger that felt unrelated to her own story, for behold her elastic skin and naturally toned calves. Even a tankini would have been an insult to such a form.

After a tin anniversary and a baby, though, she became me, and I was one snorkel away from being scuba ready.

My new suit was mega-ruched to distract from bodily ripples, its silken folds undulating like river rapids. There was also a revelatory churn in my stomach. This purchase was an inadvertent submission to my next stage of life. After exclusively relying on beachwear that could be rolled up and stuffed into a pocket, I was surrendering to mom bod.

Despite my grief, we went to the beach.

Slipping clothes over a bikini had felt no different than if it were underwear. Tugging a shirt over my postpartum drop cloth, however, was about as natural as wearing two coats. Did Clark Kent feel this clunky when he buttoned his dress shirt over his superhero costume?

We landed on the shore as a family: my husband in the same trunks he'd always worn, his physical self scarcely altered by fatherhood or time; my son, fifteen months old, too young for water adventures last summer, or perhaps his mother too timid to initiate them, now lifting his curved feet from the gritty sand in hesitant wonder; and me, eyeing the colony of Gen Zers sunbathing down the coast, boasting bandeau tops and whimsy.

Suddenly, my son took off toward the surf and I followed in pursuit—not in the alluring slow-motion jaunt of a *Baywatch* lifeguard, but in the oh-shit scramble of someone whose heart depended on keeping an impulsive, irrational, precious little maniac upright and well. I lunged for him, and hark—inside my mom uniform, I didn't have to cross an arm over my chest as I once did when diving under a wave, and, after I'd scooped him up, I didn't have to reach around to loosen a cloth scrap from my crack or pat around to make sure nothing had accidentally popped out. Everything was exactly as it should be. The sun was warm on our shoulders and I, dressed for the occasion, was not a nymph but a fierce water deity.

My creation squealed his delight. I laughed too, and together we barreled into the sea.

Clean Copy

ANNE BAGAMERY

"Can I have a dictionary?"

The hiring editor turned around and looked at me, open-mouthed.

"You want to take a spelling test . . . with a dictionary?"

"Yes." I kept my eyes on his face, trying not to let him see me sweat.

The editor chuckled. "A reporter has to be able to spell correctly," he said. "We want to test your ability to do that."

I took a beat.

"No, you want me to guess at something I don't know," I said. "If you hired me, I would never do that. I would ask someone or look it up."

Now it was his turn to take a beat.

"I probably won't need it," I continued. "I'm a good speller. But if I have any doubts, I'll look it up. And I'll turn in clean copy."

He looked down at the floor, chuckled again, and said, "I'll be right back."

• • •

Ever since I was fourteen, I had known what I wanted to do with my life.

"This is very good," my ninth-grade English teacher said, handing me back an essay. "You should write fiction."

"I don't like making things up."

"Well, then, you should be a journalist."

To fourteen-year-old me, it was a burst of light. From then on, I grabbed every opportunity I could find—from high-school newspapers to my college daily, from local correspondent for the neighborhood weekly to campus stringer for a national newsweekly.

When I snagged a magazine internship in New York the summer after my junior year of college, I felt like I had made it. For eight glamorous weeks, I did everything they asked me to do and more.

I couldn't wait to come back after graduation—as I said to my supervising editor in my exit interview when she asked me about my plans.

"You can't come back here, because you don't know anything," she said in her soft Southern accent. "You have no idea whether you can do this for more than a few weeks because you've never done it before. And you don't know what you want because you've never done anything else."

Two years at a small newspaper would be a good start, she suggested as I tried to hold back my tears. If I did well and I still wanted to come back, I could call her.

• • •

I went back to college for my senior year, determined to make that call. First, though, I had to get a newspaper job.

I sent out a ton of letters and résumés and writing samples—"clips," in journalese—and got one nibble: an interview at a small afternoon newspaper in Virginia. They had an opening for a police reporter—the classic entry-level position.

They flew me in, put me up for the night, and set up a day of interviews with the key editors. Between appointments, I sat in the newsroom and observed the reporters at work. Every one of them had a well-worn dictionary on their desk.

"Nervous?" the reporter next to me asked. I nodded.

"Don't be," he said. "If you got this far, you're fine. The last step is the spelling test."

"About that," I said. "I notice you all have dictionaries. Do you use yours?"

He did a double take. "Of course," he said. "You never guess at something you don't know. You always want to turn in clean copy."

• • •

The hiring editor brought me a dictionary. I opened it once, to check the spelling of "sarsaparilla."

Why did I do it? I probably could have passed the test without the dictionary. I also, just by asking for it, could have blown my chance at the one job offer I might get. But sitting in that newsroom, surrounded by people who I fervently hoped would be my colleagues, I felt something that has never left me: that journalism is not just a job, and that you have to do it the right way for the right reasons.

I passed the test and got the job. The hiring editor was the first in a long line of wonderful mentors I've had over the years: terse, rigorous, and fair. When I left the paper, he took me out for lunch. I asked him what it was about me that led him to offer me the job.

"It was the dictionary," he said. "You were right. And nobody else had ever asked."

In Search of the Black Female Superhero

LEIGHANN LORD

Who doesn't love female superheroes? Back in the day, I was a big fan of *Buffy the Vampire Slayer* and *Xena: Warrior Princess*. For a time I thought my silver bracelets were every bit as powerful as Wonder Woman's. She has an invisible jet. I have frequent flyer miles.

My favorite, of course, is Storm. Cue the orchestra and flash the lightning. Storm is one of the X-Men. She is a beautiful, elegant African woman with the power to control the weather. Halle Berry has played her in the movies, but I think the part should have gone to Angela Bassett, and by Angela Bassett, I mean me. But alas, I was not in the running for the role.

So, there's Storm and then there's . . . and then there's . . . hmmm. . . . Um, where are all the Black Female Superheroes? It would seem Storm is also Highlander. Can there really be only one? In frustration, but not really expecting an answer, I asked My Dad if he knew of any Black Female Superheroes, and he said, "You mean besides your mother?" When I stopped laughing, I realized he had a point.

When I was growing up, our house was the Hall of Justice, and it was easy to believe My Mother had special powers. With super strength she went to work every day, full-time, and ran a household.

My Mom didn't need Wonder Woman's truth lasso. She could tell if you were lying just by looking at you; aided, of course, by the all-seeing, all-knowing eyes in the back of her head. Xena's war whoop was but a whimper compared to my mother calling my name in her mixed Jamaican-American accent. And woe be unto me if she had to call me more than once.

My Mother had the power to transform. She was daughter, sister, wife, mother, aunt, teacher, nurse, cook, disciplinarian, friend, and, one day before she knew it, an insanely proud great-grandmother.

And so it would seem that my search for a Black Female Superhero begins and ends with she who bore me. But does it? For most of my life I thought My Mother could do it all. But the truth is, she is only human, and doing it all comes at a price. The years she spent being everything to everyone left her exhausted. Now that she is on what she calls "the down side" of her mountain, she doesn't always have the energy to do some of the things she might like to do just for herself. As she often says, "The mind is willing, but the body is weak."

And so now, without preamble or ceremony, our roles have reversed. There are some days (and by some, I mean all) when I feel like the Greatest American Hero; like I've been given powers I didn't ask for and have no idea how to use. I fear I will be John Conner at the end of *Terminator 3*, when a panicked voice on the other end of the phone asks, "Who's in charge?" And John reluctantly says, "I am."

This is nowhere near as easy as Buffy, Xena, Wonder Woman, Storm, or My Mother made it look. It occurs to me that some of the most admired superheroes never asked to be one. They are extraordinary because they rise to the role. As we used to say, "They put an 'H' on their chest and handle it."

But I see now that what's really heroic is finding the balance between helping others without losing yourself; something that all women, super or not, seem to struggle with.

Well, in the end, alzheimer's (lowercase intentional) is the evil villain in the story that came for My Mom. She/we fought for five years. We lost My Dad along the way. And I learned that true courage is fighting the everyday inglorious battles despite knowing you'll eventually lose the war.

So, I guess I'm the Highlander now.

It's hard.

But I was once loved by a superhero.

A Special Education

LAURA ROSSI

Is everybody in the world trying to get online at *exactly* the same time?

I'm standing in the middle of my kitchen in my faded plaid pajama pants and a tattered gray Las Vegas hoodie. I have a lukewarm cup of coffee in my hand, bedhead, and undereye circles the same color as the sweatshirt. Next to me, rocking in a chair that is definitely *not* a rocking chair, is my teen son, a high school junior. He has special needs, and today he officially starts "virtual learning," which is the tidy phrase parents and educators are using to describe the highly *untidy* process of schooling and education during a pandemic.

Up until recently, my son spent the school day with a highly skilled Special Education team. Now his teachers are sitting in their kitchens, living rooms, and bedrooms poised to support him through a computer screen. This is challenging for any student, but for a teen struggling with fine motor issues, auditory challenges, and social skill deficits, the situation is less than ideal—only a special educator sitting in my kitchen right now would make it ideal.

As he is logging in again and again, trying to get onto (or is it into?) his first-ever Google hangout, I realize this video platform isn't just a portal to his high school—it is a lifeline for both of us. Without his skilled team, we can't "pivot" (the most overused word of the pandemic) to homeschooling.

Today is Monday. Day one. Science class. I think. Devoted educator Ms. K is smiling brightly, and so is Mr. D (another calming presence). They are extraordinary. These teachers know my son and he loves them. They have expertise. I do not.

While my son tries to open documents, I pop my bedhead, like a bobblehead, into the video to update his teachers. Meanwhile, messages are pouring in: I'm "chatting" with my son's OT, PT, school psychologist, case manager, trying to schedule sessions. I'm furiously texting Ms. K during live class, and I must reply ASAP to the vice principal. Every person I'm interacting with is calm, pleasant, and has the word "special" in his/her title, while I'm falling apart like a day-old diner meat loaf "special."

Mornings I drink extra coffee to face the panoply of sounds in our kitchen: my son virtually high-fiving his friends, the teachers telling students to mute, iPhone/laptop notifications echoing throughout the house, our dog barking, my son's twin asking me the same question over and over, and my swearing about a call for my public relations agency. This repeats itself multiple times daily as does my mantra: I am the most "un-special" educator substitute ever. And then I grab a piece of paper and a pencil and start taking notes about the moon phases while holding a calculator for today's math class. When virtual school wraps up five hours later, I'm still in my pajamas, somehow we all had a snack *and* lunch, our heads ache, we need a nap, and everyone is grumpy.

The weekdays are one long, meandering, unending school day. We muddle through A days and B days. We live for the weekends (only different from the weekdays because we don't have school). It's Groundhog Day IRL. Screen-fatiguing tasks fill hours with no bright spots for my son—no lunch in the cafeteria with friends, no fun team sports, no bus rides, nothing.

Side by side, my son and I learn how to do spreadsheets and PowerPoint. We eat lunch as a family. We livestream music. Birds—Cardi B (the red cardinal) and Mister B (the huge blue jay)—take the place of friends and classmates. We wake up before the alarm clock. I look forward to our movement break like I used to look forward to Pilates class. My son has choreographed outfit changes for school: athletic clothes for movement breaks, casual clothes for regular class, and a blazer-shirt-tie combo for online video presentations (he learned how to "present" his screen!).

One day I wake up and can't remember the last time I felt stressed about virtual learning. The Wi-Fi panic is gone. The anxiety about the Agri-Science project magically disappeared—my son's homemade rosemary skin toner is part of my regular beauty routine now. I even learned how to make the high school cafeteria's rare "special" buffalo chicken wrap.

The once tentative birds welcome us now instead of the other way around.

Nothing has changed. Everything has changed. Every day is special. A new special.

My Zia

MARIA DECOTIS

I step onto the miniature runway in sunbaked Reggio Calabria, the crispy lush toe of the boot that is Italy. The air feels like real air, not American air (which I assume they generate in some artificial reservoir for cheap) and tastes like salt. My Zia clutches my arm like it's a threat. She's in her eighties. I'm hers now. She always wanted children, but could never have them, as the saying goes. She holds on to me like she's my seat belt. Her nephew, Antonio, drives us along steep cliffs with no rails that plummet into the Mediterranean. She works fast, talks fast, thinks even faster. Before I've even entered her one-bedroom apartment, she seems to be afraid I'll abandon her. She lives across the street from an elementary school soaked in graffiti, mostly romantic. "Ti amo, Maria" is written over and over again. I wonder if my Zia did it. She keeps me so close, hugging me with her eyes and slowing me with her food.

I have nightmares about my little cousin. I wake up in the middle of the night, and she's standing there staring at me. I'm not afraid. I know she has longing, a longing for someone she never had. I long too. She wakes me up early every morning, and I stumble outside and sleep on the beach, as God intended. I stay out until 3:00 a.m. drinking wine and philosophizing about art in abandoned amphitheaters covered in anarchy symbols. My Zia interrogates me in the morning; she forbids it, of course. I do it anyway because I'm young and I want to stick it to the MAN, whose identity is lost on me. She doesn't want to lose me. Where does she think I'll disappear to? Into the sea? I can't wait to lose myself.

From the beach, I stare at the Sfallasà Bridge. It was the third-largest bridge in the world upon its opening. It's taller than my nightmares. I think it can defeat them. I feel my little cousin's presence in the air, the cliffs, and the clouds. The bridge is close to heaven.

We watch *Il Segreto* together, a Spanish soap opera soaked with passion and deceit and everything my Zia thrives on. She tells me which men she thinks are beautiful, "Questo è bello." We have the same taste; this oddly comforts me. At dinner she tells me she had a boyfriend who was in love with her and wanted to marry her, but then he got another girl pregnant so he had to marry her instead. "But he was in love with ME," she says with an admirable self-confidence I wish I possessed. I wonder about the young men who loved my grandmother. She and my grandpa had an arranged marriage. I wish I could talk to her. Peppa had an arranged marriage too. She does like to arrange things: meetings for me with every paisano in the entire tiny town and their colossal bridge that watches over them. My little cousin is telling me something through the people here. They pass along the message through their cigarette rolled R's and espresso-flavored face kisses.

I walk on the cobblestones that reach higher and higher into the cliff trying to control it and a man on his motorino pulls up to me. "Want to have a ride?" I feel a pang of shame. I say no thanks, lower my head, and try to walk away. He won't let it go. "Vuoi fare amore?" (Want to make love?) I feel a panicked danger in my heart and walk faster. He offers me $20 for sex, and I think this is not enough money for what is being proposed, a gross miscalculation in my opinion. By the time I arrive back at my Zia's house, she's already heard about the man on the motorino and scolds me for being outside in the daylight, walking alone, while being a woman. Damn this cittadina with the news that travels like a game of telephone between the grand, sweeping gestures of women with dark hair and dark eyes and loud laughs. I know it's because she wants to protect me. But I want to protect her, from whatever tradition allows women to keep blaming ourselves for men's violence. Maybe another time; I'm tired because Zia wakes me up early. And my little cousin isn't returning. Maybe tomorrow. Maybe when I figure out who the MAN is.

Horse Girl

JULIA MARRINAN

My job blends athletic trainer, animal communicator, and professional athlete in the only Olympic sport in which men and women compete as equals. My adult life has revolved around horses; I moved states away to work and ride in an internationally competitive three-day eventing program.

And yes, "eventing" is an actual word, describing the three-pronged process where the horse and rider compete in dressage, cross-country, and show jumping. Think of it as an equestrian triathlon. Competition results obviously depend on the work you put in at home, so riders practice constantly, usually under the watchful eye of a fellow professional or trainer. Galloping at nearly four-foot-tall solid obstacles is never easy, but the more coaching you have, the better.

Physical fitness is crucial to making it around a cross-country course, but equally important is your mental toughness. The ability to make decisions under pressure and move through fear is essential to eventing, whether it's picking your distances while moving at twenty miles per hour or maintaining a forward ride during your dressage test when your horse is terrified of going near the judge. It's understandable—you wouldn't be thrilled at getting scored out loud and in public, either.

Being in public is a big part of the routine, even on so-called average days.

On an average day, I ride seven horses. If it's hot, I'll take my helmet off in between, but if it's humid, and especially if I know we're having owners visit the barn, I'll leave my helmet on. If asked, I would claim it's for the sake of professionalism, but in truth it's mostly because "helmet hair" makes "hat hair" look positively stylish.

Sometimes, though, a little vanity can be a good thing.

Last winter, I was walking down the aisle to get to my next ride when a horse in the courtyard got loose. The sudden motion from outside spooked the horse in front of me, and—reacting through fear—he kicked out with both of his hind legs.

In the business, we call that a "double barrel."

Even though I was off to the side, one hoof struck me hard, and I mean hard, in the head. His other hoof hit my side. The impact lifted me off my feet and launched me into the air. When I landed, it was with two broken ribs, a severely lacerated spleen, a split lip, and a splitting headache to match. I later learned the headache was an indication of my traumatic brain injury. The helmet saved my life.

If I hadn't been worried about my hair, I might not have made it; don't let anybody tell you not to follow your instincts when it comes to fashion that just might save your life.

Rushed by ambulance to a regional hospital, one large enough to handle the complexity of my injuries, I spent three days in a trauma unit.

I was unable to sit up. I was also unable to remember anything for more than fifteen minutes. Three days was a long time for someone who started asking to be let out of the ambulance halfway through the ride.

And if you think having broken ribs is hard, try convincing nurses to get you a cup of coffee when they think you're a pediatric patient. Most wings of the hospital were filled with coronavirus patients, so any non-Covid-positive patients under age thirty were placed in the pediatric unit. My sheets had tigers on them, my spirometer had monkeys on it, and my breakfast menu had a serious absence of caffeine.

I spent the next few weeks in bed making contingency plans: What could I do to make sure that nothing like that would ever happen again? Eventing is a high-risk sport: Horses are innately kind creatures, but they still weigh a thousand pounds and are unpredictable—especially highly fit, highly flighty competition horses.

The skills I developed when I was riding competitively were exactly what helped me to literally get back on the horse: I was determined not to let fear stop me from doing something I love.

Still, I ratcheted my safety levels up from "doesn't take any risks" to "verges on paranoid." With patience, planning, and medical guidance, I was riding again as soon as I safely could, fiercely determined to stay a horsewoman—the helmet hair will just have to do.

Peanut Butter and Jelly

NICOLE CATARINO

It's just a peanut butter and jelly sandwich.

Simple. Easy. I've made a hundred of these before, and I'll make a thousand more in my lifetime. The entire process will take me two minutes max, three if I can't get the lid off the jelly jar right away. All I have to do is pack this lunch so my family and I can take a trip to a park along the shoreline, enjoy the nice weather, and celebrate Father's Day. It's fine. I can do this. *It's just a sandwich.*

I repeat this to myself over and over again, run the words through my head and over my tongue, but nothing seems to convince my trembling hands otherwise. They still won't move. Cold hardwood floor beneath my sweaty feet, I stand frozen in the kitchen, fingers hovering over the handle to the freezer, completely incapable of yanking it open. My whole body trembles, head to toe, like a leaf in a tropical storm, and with the weight of each breath, my chest shudders as I sob. Try as I might, I cannot get the bread from the fridge.

Of course it's not the peanut butter and jelly sandwich that's making me shake. It's the fact that if I make this sandwich, I've committed myself to going to the park along the shoreline with crowds of strangers and no running water (or clean restrooms) for several hours on end. The very concept has terrified me so badly that my brain skipped the "fight or flight" response and went straight for paralysis. Which is why I am empty-handed and sandwich-less.

I've harbored this panic, this ability to make monsters out of molehills, for as long as I can remember. When I was six, I couldn't use the bathroom by myself in fear that the entire building would erupt into flame the second I locked myself into a stall. When I was twelve, the very idea of contracting an illness would send me into frenzies of hand sanitizer application and warm-water washing. At fifteen I picked up the habit of knocking on every inch of any wooden surface within reach for luck, so frequently that my knuckles would be scarlet by the day's end. Eighteen saw panic attacks sparking asthma attacks in bathrooms or bustling dorm rooms, and each subsequent year saw much of the same. Each time, I would scratch my scalp raw with carefully manicured nails and clench my fists so tight that half-moons scar my palms. Every day, my body grows sore from the compulsive impulses and tics that overtake me as I obey whatever my mind demands to calm the storms of my anxiety.

But it's manageable; it's tolerable—only because I force it to be so. I take the reins and sculpt my outward appearance in a way that ensures I'm told I seem "so put-together all the time!" more than I'm ever asked if I'm okay. With both hands, I gather whatever semblance of control I can find in every other aspect of my life and hope that "fake it until you make it" will carry me through the tempest. After a while, a pattern emerged: Wake up, power through, and hope the next day will be easier.

Then twenty saw the pandemic, and the worst mental state I had ever been in.

Which brings me to twenty-one, where I stand over my kitchen counter and will my hands to *open the damn freezer* because I will not be the one to ruin Father's Day by letting this get the better of me. After all, the only reason I'm crying as I stand in front of the fridge is because no one else is home. I will have wiped my tears, stilled the tremors, and steadied my voice by the time my parents arrive, because I will never let anyone else see me like this, despite the fact that *this* is more me than the person everyone thinks has all their ducks in a row.

The freezer will eventually open. The sandwich will get made. A compromise will be struck, and we will all travel to a little shopping town instead with running water and fewer strangers. I will tell no one what happened, and I will eat lunch with a mixture of triumph and deep relief.

And the next day will be the same as always: Wake up, power through, and hope that, one day, it will get easier.

Freak Paralysis

SUZETTE MARTINEZ STANDRING

A freak paralysis began my pandemic version of "how I spent my summer vacation."

I was in the kitchen, peeling an orange, when suddenly my right leg went numb. Dropping to the floor, I yelled, "What's happening?! What's happening?!"

I had no previous symptoms or problems. Just boom! On the floor, my orange rolling away from me.

What to do?

EMTs might batter down my front door.

"Oh, no, doors are too expensive to replace."

So commando-style, I crawled to unlock it and called 9-1-1.

The medics expected to find a stroke victim, but they found me confused but chirpy-normal, except for my dead leg.

At the ER, my paralysis lasted for five hours. Many doctors had a look-see, and I had a friendly conversation with one. *What a nice bedside manner,* I thought, until he said, "Well, mental illness isn't obvious."

The conclusion from later MRIs, X-rays, tests, and a neurologist?

"You are a medical anomaly."

But an MRI of my thoracic region revealed a lung tumor, unrelated to my temporary paralysis.

The doctor said, "The size (3.6 cm) suggests cancer. It needs immediate removal."

My mind reeled with a zillion things to do, and now surgery topped the list.

As a way to stay calm, I had a Reiki treatment, which is a form of positive energy transfer. During it, I felt a buzz go through my body, and then a feeling of profound peace.

But this is the thing about holistic practices. They can lead to self-examination and change.

After working on me, the Reiki practitioner noted: "You have a schedule that would kill most people."

"Do I?"

She said, "Your busyness did not cause this lung tumor, but it's a metaphor. You run from thing to thing and you can barely catch your breath. You need to slow way down."

What? How?

It was time to offload guilt, obligation, stress, and pressure. Post-surgery, they had to be kept at bay.

Aside from the expectations of others, what part did my own ego play in not letting go? Am I the only person in the world who can do what I do?

Yes! I am the only one who really cares about getting it done right!

Pause.

OK, fine. There are others.

Pause.

But I don't like to let go and delegate.

Then a terrible realization:

Oh, dear God, I'm totally dispensable.

Then a wee inner voice: *You don't have to keep racing around like a gerbil set afire in a bathtub. You have a choice, you know.*

But dare I do things differently?

I resigned from my job; and for all my resistance based on disappointing others or being a quitter, it proved easier than I thought.

I played the cancer card. Nobody questions the cancer card.

I thought lung surgery would be a breeze. Get in, get out, tumor gone. One friend said, "Breezy? You mean operating on the organ you breathe with?"

I said, "Stop programming me for terror!"

Good news. Though the tumor proved cancerous, removal was complete, and no further treatment was needed.

But I was so naive about post-surgery pain!

Every tiny movement sent shockwaves the first three days.

Once, when David was putting me into bed, I screamed, "I can't do this! It hurts too much. I gotta stop!"

He said, "No! No! Think about Star and the girls! I can't live without you. Don't give up, Suze!"

Who's giving up? He was scooching me over too fast, that's all. No hemlock needed.

David was a strict Guardian of My Galaxy throughout my recovery.

"What are you doing, Suze?"

"I'm putting sheets in the washer."

"Put those down and get back to bed!"

The world was on a collective lockdown, and I had time to be grateful.

For things like, "At least I'm not missing anything."

But that's small stuff.

The big-ticket item was a freak paralysis that led to the early resolution of cancer. (A reason was never found, and the paralysis never returned.) Gratitude for a devoted husband and family, the outpouring of prayers from friends, as well as the courage to turn a part of my life around.

The pandemic brought the rare gift of time to make very different decisions and to create very different memories.

And don't we all have some doozies.

Life Coach

EBONY MURPHY-ROOT

In the spring of my thirty-eighth year, I muster up the courage to contact a life coach. We have a lot of acquaintances in common, mostly women writers I know from social media.

"Make more money being you!" is her promise. I want in.

Life coaching, I know, is not therapy. I've spent years in therapy and thousands in co-pays, talking through my life.

My choices? Pretty good ones: After college I taught teen moms, case-managed kids in foster care, landed a job in Manhattan, fled to Ojai at age thirty-three to work in a boarding school. Yet after trying Vipassana meditation, Reiki, and after deciding that I don't want children, I find myself unsettled.

Is that surprising for a Type B, millennial Black woman?

I want to know. So in March of 2021, as the pandemic pace bumps back to slightly more normal, I'm walking near the beach with a life coach who is known for gently encouraging women to become their best selves.

"I don't have a PhD or a podcast or a book or a lake house. I feel like an underachiever," I tell her as I try to remain breezy. "I graduated from college seventeen years ago and can't imagine how everyone else get so much done." I am thinking of high school classmates who have a thriving law practice, an MBA, and a second home in Maine.

The life coach is a slight, serious woman with dark hair, flawless skin, and a little smile, and she squints as I explain that I know I'm not living up to my potential. My first-grade teacher, Sister Ursula, warned my puzzled young parents that would happen way back when I was secretly reading under my desk. I got a "C" in conduct even though I got an "A" in everything else.

I share with the life coach, who is shorter than I imagined, my wishes and needs: I want to finish my website, enroll in yoga certification, then draft and sell my memoir.

The life coach focuses her squint, as if she is trying to see if I have imposter syndrome or perfectionism or perhaps body dysmorphia.

"But WHY do you want more?" she probes. "How much time do you spend on social media? How are your relationships with your friends? How's your marriage?"

Isn't she supposed to help me figure out where I want to be, not tell me that I don't know the difference between Facebook connections and friends?

(Are male clients given the same advice, I wonder? "Stop trying for more. Do you have friends? Work on your marriage! Stay away from Twitter!")

What I hear is, "What's so special about YOU?"

I've heard that question my entire life, asked figuratively or literally, by people who did not appreciate my working-class Black girl quirky confidence. What's special about me is that my mother, who died of fast-moving breast cancer when she was only thirty-nine years old, passed right before I graduated from high school. I want to say that I fear her story will always be my story, and that I'll always be nothing more than that girl whose mom dies right when her own life is getting started.

If I hadn't spent so much of my early youth grieving, I wonder, actively grieving as I fumbled into womanhood, succeeding outwardly on many levels but unable to reassure myself, would I be better now?

I say none of that.

"How old are you?" the life coach inquires. I breathe in deeply.

"Thirty-eight."

"Mmmm." She is squinting again.

Mmmm? What does that mean? I'm too old? Too young? I'm pathetic?

Look, I want to say: I make a decent salary by teaching—a job I find meaningful and at which I excel. I'm married to a true-hearted Mets fan who has a Public Policy degree and shares my politics. I serve on the boards of service and feminist organizations. I have had the same best friend since Sister Ursula's class. I drive a terrific car.

I leave the session wondering if I'm mistaken in wanting to be better than "good enough"—or even "just okay"?

A few days later the life coach emails me to schedule a follow-up appointment. I thank her, but I'm not meeting with her again. With her, I felt small, dumb, and diminished.

I don't need anybody to tell me not to keep hoping, wanting, doing, and being more. I say none of that.

"That makes sense," she writes. I imagine her squinting as she types.

Women and Children First

LESLIE MORGAN STEINER

"Is that an airplane, Poppa?" the girl in the window seat in front asked the man next to her. We were flying from Albuquerque to Chicago on a Friday afternoon.

At her age, I adored my father and brother. I did not know that men commit over 80 percent of violent crimes. That fifteen million children are abused annually in the United States. That three women are killed each day by the men in their lives. I trusted every male neighbor, coach, toy store clerk, and janitor, oblivious to the invisible hierarchy that places men first, women next, and children last.

I had a partial view of the girl, so tiny her feet couldn't reach the tray table. Her hair was in French-braid pigtails, fuzzy, with blonde wisps escaping. She held a stuffed kitten in her lap.

"Get your fingers out of my water," the man spit with such venom, I flinched in my seat.

A minute later: "Shut up. I'm watching my show."

I leaned forward. The girl was so quiet I thought she was holding her breath. Her hand gripped the stuffed kitten.

The man lunged to his left. A tiny voice broke through the engine noise. "Poppa, you HURT me." She started to cry. No one on the packed plane even looked up.

"I'm teaching her manners," he barked when I choked out a protest. "None of your business."

He held his body tight, as if keeping the wrath inside until it was safe to unleash it. He had no idea how familiar that body language was to me.

At twenty-two, fresh out of Harvard, wearing miniskirts and writing essays for *Seventeen* magazine about teen runaways and eating disorders, I fell for a handsome Ivy League graduate I met on the subway. He'd dropped out of eighth grade to escape his stepfather's beatings. He clawed his way to college, where professors and Wall Street recruiters recognized his rough promise. I loved him more for all that he had overcome.

Five days before our wedding, my alleged soulmate strangled me in a fury more shocking than his hands around my throat. My love faltered, but held steady. Commitment jitters, right? I slipped on my mother's lace gown and married him in Harvard Memorial Church. Soon, he was holding a Colt .45 to my temple and deciding whether I could wear makeup. Our final night together, he ripped off my clothes, broke my favorite wedding picture over my head, and strangled me into unconsciousness. He screamed obscenities and kicked me until his rage ran dry. Then he cried. Apologized. Left the apartment. As the door banged shut, I dialed 9-1-1 for the first, and last, time in my marriage.

I leaned toward the airplane window.

"I like your kitten. What's her name?"

Instead of answering, she asked, "Are those airplanes?"

She pointed to the sailboats dotting Lake Michigan in the afternoon sunshine. Her favorite color was purple. The kitten's name was Kiki. She told me she liked my hair, reaching through the back of the seats to put her small palms on my head, as if blessing me.

He hit her twice more before we got off the plane.

After six nights of worry, I drove to the airport police station. Breaking the silence about abuse is not easy—nothing about stopping abuse is easy. But the Federal Child Abuse Prevention and Treatment Act mandates that law enforcement investigate "any recent act or failure to act on the part of a parent or caregiver that results in death, serious physical or emotional harm, sexual abuse, or exploitation." Our laws, our politicians, the police—our entire society—agree that abuse, of anyone, is wrong. That bystanders should say something when we see something.

The officer had never recorded a child abuse complaint. After thanking me, he said neither the police nor the FBI would pursue this case, because "thirty seconds of bad parenting doesn't constitute cruelty, ma'am."

Shouldn't reporting child abuse be easier than getting away with it?

There are exceptional men, of course: The policemen who came when I called 9-1-1. The judge who granted my restraining order. The locksmith who arrived in twenty minutes. My divorce attorney. My twenty-four-year-old son, who is caring to all women, including me.

Over time, I hope more men will prove worthy of women's and children's trust. Until then, we need to be fierce, to break the silence against abuse however we can.

I never found out what happened to the girl on the plane.

Why Women Kill

PAMELA KATZ

My father fled Nazi Germany. On my mother's side, they ran from Russian pogroms.

Instead of being grateful for my privileged American life, the dangers that plagued my ancestors became a challenge I yearned to face. As if life isn't worth living unless someone tries to take it away.

I recognized a kindred spirit in Monika Ertl.

The forces rumbling within her were different and far stronger than mine: Her father, known as "Hitler's Photographer," made films for Leni Riefenstahl and the Führer. There was no place for an unrepentant Nazi propagandist in post-war Germany, and an outraged Hans Ertl took his wife and children into exile in La Paz, Bolivia—a dizzying and beautiful city twelve thousand feet above the sea. A place where, ironically, brutal dictators were still thriving.

For Monika, the twisted rope of evil, extending from Germany through the United States and forming a noose around Latin America, was right before her eyes. The child of a Nazi conspirator, she was determined to help rescue her adopted country from the gallows.

Ultimately, she was willing to pull a trigger to take a stand.

At fifteen, Monika eagerly followed her father into the jungle, where he taught her how to use a camera, canoe down the Amazon, and shoot a gun. Desperate to belong, she learned the languages and rituals of the Quechua and the Aymaran natives they filmed; she was pained when she saw their land and Incan treasures being stolen and destroyed.

Hans unintentionally trained his daughter to become the perfect guerrilla.

At fifteen, I became an enthusiastic backpacker. I enjoyed the beauty of the mountains and cooking over an open fire. I thought I was learning how to survive in the wild. I had no idea.

Monika was thirty when Che Guevara was killed in Bolivia. Inspired by his electrifying effect on the world, she joined the throng of followers that multiplied after his martyr's death. She hid guerrillas in her house, robbed a bank, and procured arms. She was a welcome recruit, one who could, in her adoring father's words, *shoot like a man.*

In 1971, she got her chance.

Roberto "Toto" Quintanilla, head of Bolivian Intelligence, was despised for his role in the death of Che. Two years later, he brutally tortured and murdered Che's successor, Inti Peredo, a man who was briefly, if fiercely, the love of Monika's life. It was time for a political assassination.

Toto thought he'd be safe in a sleepy post across the ocean. But the Bolivian Consul in Germany was the ideal place for Monika to do the deed. Donning a gray wig and hiding a pistol in her blue shoulder bag, she shot Quintanilla three times in the chest.

She was thirty-three. That's when I had my first baby, and worried about combining work and motherhood. A noble enough goal, but honestly, I was also concerned about losing weight.

She'd never killed before and found no joy in seeing him writhe and bleed. Monika focused on the Bolivian painting of Lake Titicaca behind his desk, the legendary home for the gold of El Dorado. She vowed that Toto's death would save lives—save a country—right a thousand wrongs.

A worldwide manhunt ensued, but Monika bravely led the fight for two more years in Bolivia before they gunned her down in the streets of La Paz.

Monika's legacy is steeped in the lie that she shot Quintanilla to avenge her lover. This cliché is comforting: Women who kill for love are passionately romantic. Women who kill for ideological commitment are terrifying.

The important woman behind the fairy tale can only emerge by shattering the condescending myths that obscure the significance of her life. She's inspired four novels, always portrayed as a gorgeous, gun-wielding guerrilla—often the lucky author's lover. She's Patty Hearst and then some.

And *then some* is the only thing they got right.

Monika's life was influenced by a potent blend of Nazi past and Bolivian present. Sired by "Hitler's Photographer," she ended as Che's devoted guerrilla. Her actions demand that we confront the violent world in which someone like her came to be.

Two exiles from opposite sides of history, I inherited the fears, and she the guilt, of our families. Monika had the courage I crave, but since my ancestors fought hard to survive, I cannot willingly choose to die for my convictions. I must live to vanquish the painful past that haunts me still, and I begin by telling her story.

Butter Knives

PATRICIA WYNN BROWN

I suppose, being a potential murderer at the age of five might give you the wrong impression of me. But here it is.

What happened was this: I grew up with a PTSD dad home from WWII, totally mentally disabled. He fought with my mom, resulting in much screaming and crying. Even as a little child I would enter the fray and Shirley Temple–style stomp and shout, "Stop hurting mommy!"

When Dad was having a "well period," he was funny, handsome, a storyteller, a beautiful singer, an artist, a photographer, and never knew a stranger. Those times were too few, and his many absences to the VA hospital and psychiatric wards left a gap and mayhem reprieve. We were NEVER to speak of our home quagmire to anyone. My telling this now is a fierce violation of our family omertà.

I do have favorite memories of my dad. He would put me in his bicycle basket that had the patchwork wool knitted quilt I nestled into. We would happily sail around the neighborhood.

It was such a hoot when he took his parachute out onto the street on a windy day and pretended he had just jumped from an airplane. The problem was, the wind actually began to make him ascend, so our next-door neighbor, George Phillips, had to tackle him and pull in the parachute.

It was typical of Dad that on one trip to the VA hospital in Chillicothe, Ohio, a stray piglet waddled on the side of the road. Dad made them stop the car and had my mom promise she would see to the squealing pink orphan. She did.

I went in the kitchen one day to find a pretty teenage girl weeping. My mom and dad were talking to her. My dad had departed his home away from home, The Keg Room, and discovered the forlorn teen wet and shivering on the street. She was a runaway. My mom fed her, and my dad made a call and returned her home.

My dad taught me to fish, frog gig, hunt, ride a bike, sing, tell stories, draw, and dance. Mom sometimes made him take me with him to the bar for her maternal relief. He would plop wee-me up onto the smoke-filled bar with a 7 Up and a pretty colored straw. I loved the war stories from the vets.

Even so, Dad's anger and violence were dynamite to my vulnerable child-self, and so I became fierce. I decided to take action.

I enlisted the assistance of my little brother. I was five, little brother was three. My dad had been hurting my mom again, she was pleading for mercy. I knew I had to do something. I was a determined child. (When I was around two, they told me, I bit my Grandma Aggie on the butt at the grocery store when she refused my toy request.)

I made a plan. I went into the kitchen of our small tract house on the working-class west side of Columbus, 2659 Eakin Road. My phone number was beautiful: Broadway 9-8305, and probably why I became a performer.

Out of the silverware drawer I chose two butter knives. I gave one to my little brother (L. B.) and I kept one. I positioned L. B. and me behind the green leather easy chair in the living room. I told L. B. to crouch down with me and hide, and we would wait for Dad to come out, butter knife daggers at the ready.

I told L. B., "We gotta kill Daddy."

It was my mission to save Mom and all of us. We had a baby sister. I encountered a snag. L. B. refused to go along with me, he being three and all, and not developing the fierce skill that I had.

Dad came out of the bedroom. I can still see him looming over us. I could not figure out how to start killing him because it was a good dad morning. He smiled his broad Irish smile and said, "What are you doing back there?" L. B. just looked at him. I offered the universal subterfuge answer: "Nothing."

Dad took the butter knives, shaking his head like *you crazy kiddies*, and walked them back into the kitchen, not knowing he was just seconds from being murdered.

Dad's mental health continued to deteriorate, ending in his horrible news-making death at age sixty. We were spared. Others were not. I still have the butter knives.

In Loving Reference to Ire

ANGELA AISEVBONAYE

My anger gets shit done.

Not my pride, not my drive, not my altruism. Not my intellect, not my affability, not even my fear of failure. No, it's my incandescent dissatisfaction with whatever undesired status quo I face that compels me to look forward, wipe away the tears, and reach a key conclusion: Oh *hell* no! I am NOT having this!

In my twenty-six years, I've found that sadness is a form of paralysis. It interlaces with my mind; ensnaring and snuffing out my hopes, goals, and intentions; leaving me with a single, fervent wish: that it, whatever *it* is, would all just go away. But it never does, because misery has a curious way of overstaying its welcome, inviting all its pals (Hello, guilt and self-loathing! What's up, avoidance?) to live in your mind rent-free while dishes and noise complaints pile up, unaddressed.

And indeed, throughout my mostly unhappy college experience, melancholy and its ne'er-do-well friends proved to be horrid tenants.

As a heavily-sheltered seventeen-year-old, with no money or anywhere else to go, I tried and failed to push myself through a nursing program and a college that my loving but controlling STEM career–obsessed parents had chosen for me. When I later failed out of nursing school, computer science was their next choice. As a lonely nineteen-year-old with abysmal self-esteem, I escaped an abusive relationship that ended with my ex's suicidal threats and my subsequent calls to the police. As a depressed twenty-year-old who wanted nothing more than to move on, I was drugged with Xanax and date-raped by a man whose real name I still don't know.

At these and every other downward turn my life took then, misery enveloped me, precluding action and incurring increasingly higher costs, like weight gain, hair loss, failing grades, and revoked financial aid. Only by the skin of my teeth did I graduate at twenty-three, with a cobbled-together general studies degree and a transcript littered with Fs. But I made it through, and that degree, despite the record of shoddy academic performance it represented, also signified freedom: freedom from my parents' choices, freedom from this horrible chapter, and, especially, freedom from depressive immobility.

And so anger became the vehicle through which I *got shit done*. I knew my grades would seriously reduce my employment prospects. But armed with my degree, newfound confidence in my ability to thrive, and the reading I *finally* had time to do after graduating, I bathed myself in fury. All this time I've spent, this debt I'm in, the iniquities I've suffered, the fucking loony, detrimental shit our leaders get up to in Washington and on Wall Street, and I'm just here, posted up in my parents' house merely reading about all the problems I could be out there solving, and watching the lives I could be living on TV?

Not this time. You guessed it: I was NOT having it!

I got so angry that I spent twelve straight hours every day searching for a full-time job and submitting over three hundred applications until I got a call center job in insurance IT.

Upon starting, discovering firsthand the extent to which I despise the corporate world, and watching my boyfriend go to law school to study what I've yearned to learn all these years, I became so furious that I quit what was a well-paying job with excellent benefits to matriculate *again* as a broke undergraduate, taking a part-time campus job in the hopes of improving my grades and ultimately working for the public, not some moron with millions of dollars. I approached coursework with a renewed, even ardent diligence, going without, commuting and staying at school for (again) twelve hours a day, because I didn't just want a degree. *I wanted As, so I got them.* And I still do.

By this time, it was my destitution enraging me: I work and study hard, and excel; I spend so much, and for what? Another fucking undergrad degree? I was so pissed, I attended information sessions and started drafting my personal essay. I wrathfully completed the application for a graduate program in public administration; my fury saw me through the GRE, and I was soon accepted into the program of my dreams.

Replacing my woe with ire invigorated and bolstered me for action and real, meaningful change. My anger, in its refusal to leave me idle, saved me from the paralysis of misery and set me free.

I am forever grateful.

Maybe-Visions

AMY WHIPPLE

On a summer-sweaty Saturday morning in late September, I push my son's wheelchair along Pittsburgh's uneven sidewalks toward our neighborhood playground. We pass a women's consignment shop, its window displaying a chocolate brown hat (*Perhaps vintage?* I think): A thin leather strip circles the base, anchoring three felted flowers along the front. I consider buying it for one of my church ladies before my brain screeches to a comic, cosmic halt.

That, I realize, *is the hat from the vision.* Well, maybe a vision. Really, a glimpse at best.

At the playground, I push my son on the swing with one hand and text my friends with the other: *Say I had what may or may not have been a vision seven years ago, and the hat from that maybe-vision is in a store window. I check it out, right?*

You absolutely check it out, they respond.

● ● ●

At twenty-nine years old, I glimpsed myself on the stairs in my parents' Virginia house. I am thin, svelte even—physiologically impossible for some-one who comes from hardy peasant stock and psychologically improbable for someone who thunders through life—wearing a brown suit, three-quarter-length sleeves, slight brown belt around my waist. The suit (Is it made of tweed? What exactly is tweed?) reminds me more of my beloved, sturdy Lucy Ricardo than the Beltway's beloved, sophisticated Ann Taylor. And I'm wearing the hat.

I was, in real life, two years into a five-ish-year depression, two months into the first of three rounds of intensive treatment. The noise in my head is symphonic, a mix of loud, layered madness. I feared I would soon have to admit defeat—why, I can no longer tell you—and move home; this flash, I assumed, was me returning from, perhaps, a government contractor job, headed toward my lavender-walled bedroom and its twin-size Laura Ashley bedspread, a life I aggressively did not want.

A few days later, I was at church on the first blustery and bleary autumn day, volunteering ("volunteering"?) for an event. After four years of noncommittal attendance, I had made the mistake of introducing myself, which, in the Presbyterian Church, is the end of your committee-less days. I walked downstairs into the kitchen for the first time and stepped into the collective memory of over one hundred years of women—a feeling that I had been there many times before and would be many times in the future. That there would be a future.

The possible future, by way of the past, emanated from enviable cabinets full of formidable flowered dinner plates and a shelf holding towers of scratched muffin tins, heavy drawers of mismatched silverware, and piles of peach tablecloths to wash. I saw myself decades later, effortlessly guiding some event the way I effortlessly guided children with my fingertips gentle between their shoulder blades.

I conflated the hat and the kitchen and turned them into harbingers of survival. And spent another three years doubting, having a difficult time believing in a life without the chaos in my brain, parallel scabs on my skin, the exhaustive tension of eat-don't-eat-how-much-space-do-I-should-I-take-up.

● ● ●

Friend-affirmation in hand, I decide I'll buy the hat if it's $50 or less—and also know I'm unlikely to walk away if it's more. But it's only $35 and . . . from Anthropologie.

I don't know what to do with having hung my metaphorical hat on Anthropologie, a store I'm older than and thus one unlikely to provide a multigenerational lesson in perseverance. Laughing, I buy it and balance it on a corner of the bookcase in my bedroom.

I find the glimpse/maybe-vision in my journal: "If there isn't a hat, there could be." *If?* I don't know what to do with having hung my literal hat on *could be*. Except I hung my life on *could be*. How else would I escape madness's ferocity other than by persisting with each decision throughout each day in hopes of finding what could be?

And I did. I found a medication that created solid ground. Used therapeutic skills. Stayed on the planet (and in Pittsburgh). Joined committees. Met my son. Changed jobs. Continued to not own a suit or move gracefully or say the right things. One day, I sat down at my desk and could actually work. Cook dinner and eat it. Hear the alarm and get out of bed after the first snooze (mostly).

It all seemed as unlikely as receiving a vision, maybe or not, if or could be, but was as real as the hat balanced on the bookcase behind me.

Whatever Happens Just Does

RYAN WILTZIUS

I switch positions on top of my sloppily made bed and realize with disgust that the spot where I've been sitting is saturated with thigh-sweat. Great. This duvet cover was expensive. I'm willing to bet it can't be washed at the laundromat.

I catch myself inadvertently clenching my jaw. I catch myself doing this a few times. Probably why I've been getting headaches.

It's strange to live long enough to realize my body is capable of doing whatever it wants, for any reason, at any time. I massage my sore cheeks and temples, hoping for some relief; they are tender to the touch.

Does anyone really have a clear vision of themselves beyond thirty?

Before they turn thirty, I mean.

I learned this trick in a meditation app: Flutter your eyes closed, take a few deep breaths. In through your nose, out through your mouth. Begin to notice The Sounds around you. Detach one from all the rest. Identify it, separate it. Do it again, again . . . again.

Eventually you yourself soften and dissolve. You are only a part of this collection of sounds. Usually this process placates me, but tonight the street is full of fireworks and celebration. I feel small, and unimportant.

I read once that the words "noise" and "nausea" share the same Latin root. Exposure to constant noise causes blood to heat, boil.

I struggle to sever my own thoughts from the cacophony. I can't hear myself think.

I breathe in and pick out the constant sputtering fuzz of the air conditioner. Its occasional wheeze, a wet crackle. I breathe out. A lively jazz horn, Louis Prima, from the living room where my boyfriend, Matt, is watching a movie with our dog on the couch in the dark. *The Jungle Book*. Something about it always manages to temporarily quell the chaos.

Tomorrow is his mom's birthday. Kathy. She'd be turning fifty-nine.

When we were nineteen, the first weeks of July were salt, sun, and ocean. Beach soccer, cousins, makeshift beds and shared rooms, icebox birthday cakes, cans of Diet Coke held upright in the sand. Late-night card games with aunts and uncles. Exploring the dunes, finding an enormous whelk, finally catching the wave you can ride right down, all the way onto the beach. We squished into the lifeguard's chair and I tucked my knees up into a borrowed sweatshirt. Our eyes, bright and unblinking, reflected fireworks.

• • •

I breathe in and pick out fireworks, like gunshots, set off in the street outside my window.

I, myself, do not technically have a monetizable skill. At best, I am like an exotic pet no one knows how to play with and can't afford to feed.

Still, the only way I am able to understand anything at all is to pour out the contents of the vessel. Detach each thing from all the others. I pick up pieces, rearrange, glue back together, make a Frankenstein's monster. I sing a little song. I rip out anything that makes me feel anything. The ripping itself feels like catharsis.

I am trying to figure out the purpose of my corporeal form, of place, of time, of suffering, of love, of purpose itself. Okay? It isn't easy!

Ask anyone with this fire in their belly, they'll tell you: "It is enough to drive you fucking crazy."

Everyone must feel fucking crazy, at this point—right?

I take myself apart, folding back a paper people chain of past selves. I really look at them, one at a time.

How old are we when we learn that life is hard? That it isn't fair? How many people learn this at fifteen . . . thirteen . . . ten years old? I remember becoming aware of my own ugliness in the fourth grade. Self-conscious and apologetic about my physical existence since the fourth grade.

I have lost so much that sometimes it feels opaque, like I cannot see beyond it or there is nothing else to see. When I think I am absolutely certain of this, though, the light hits just right. Something glints, underneath. Something golden. It winks at me.

Inside, so many of us are survivors. Models of bravery, heroism, and strength who bore the weight and carried us to the other side. Shouldn't that work be worth something in the end?

I don't want to mourn my past anymore, wishing things were different or that I'd done things differently. These are fruitless wishes. Instead, this Record of Becoming: a testament to my Self, the one I owe my life; the lion-hearted girl.

Just Say YES

CINDY EASTMAN

One day, I got a text from a former colleague. She asked me if I was interested in coming back to teach a couple of English classes at the local community college for the next semester. A little background to this question: I had been "let go" several years earlier at the whim of an administrator, ostensibly because there weren't any classes to assign me, despite already being listed in the course catalog. This administrator once handed me an award for teaching, so it was a bit of a shock when the school simply stopped assigning classes to me. A couple of years after that, I was at a school event and one of my friends asked if I was available to teach—and I happily reapplied. I was given two classes for the next semester, only to be sidelined again—by the same woman. Then, the aforementioned text. That administrator had retired and would I be interested in coming back? I didn't hesitate—I answered yes.

Conventional wisdom has been telling us women for years to "Just say no." No is the power we were given. Tell him no. Tell them no. Say no to unwanted facial hair, say no to unacceptable pay, say no to icky manhandling on the first date. Stand up for yourselves, assert yourself. Be the dame you want to see in the world. And we did . . . we asserted and insisted and persisted and we said no, No, NO! But I'm beginning to think there's also power in saying yes. Uttering a firm "Yes" is quite liberating. "Yes" is "I want that" rather than "No, don't do that to me."

I now believe that "yes" gives me more control over the choices that show up in my life.

I said yes to my old teaching job even though the previous two experiences had been painful, humiliating, and devastating to my career. I walked away from it—both times—without making a fuss, because teaching was doing something I loved. I had met people I stayed connected to long after I left the school and I discovered work I was good at. My pride was urging me to say no; it suggested I run screaming in the opposite direction from this déjà vu offer. What if it was taken away again?

But what if it wasn't? If I said no, I'd never know. By saying yes, I had the opportunity to explore what I wanted the outcome to be rather than let it stay in the hands of those who didn't know me from the next adjunct on the list. When I said yes, it gave me the chance to learn more about what I want and define how I want to go about getting it. It could all go sideways—in fact, there are definitely times when I probably should have stuck with no. But that gave me information too. And isn't that what life is all about? Getting information from this experience so we can apply it to the next one? Saying yes gives us the information we'd never have if we say no.

Yes and no aren't black and white. There's a scale—as with everything in life—of when and where one is more appropriate than the other. You'll still need a resounding "No" in your repertoire, as well as a good solid "Yes" without qualification. Yes doesn't require cleverness or self-deprecation. We (or maybe it's just me) can camouflage a yes in apology with our eyes closed. Our (or maybe it's just mine) texted and emailed yeses are populated with cheery-faced emojis or are wishy-washy in their resolve (yes, if you're sure and you don't mind and if it's not a bother).

So, say yes. Yes. A thousand times yes! Develop your yes muscle with frequent workouts. Channel your inner Meg Ryan in *When Harry Met Sally* and announce, "Yes, I will take that promotion. Yes, I will have another glass of wine. Yes, I am going away for the weekend with my friend (or by myself)." No demurring, no trade-offs, no nothing. Just a simple, unhesitating yes.

Walking the Tightrope

LISA CHAU

I have had a very privileged life, even as a woman of color. I was raised by supportive grandparents who genuinely cared about my happiness. I graduated from a magnet high school and earned degrees from top-tier colleges. I have been in long-term relationships where I felt completely safe and loved. My home addresses have included zip codes from upscale neighborhoods. My passports collect stamps from great international trips to Asia and Europe. My CV is a long list of credible accomplishments, volunteer work, and testimonials.

This list is the same reason it's difficult for me to reveal the following: I've been struggling since 2010. That's the year my beloved paternal grandfather passed, and the same year I left my second fiancé.

At first, I felt adrift, unmoored and without direction. Later, I felt as if I were constantly teetering on a tightrope with no safety net.

I don't have imposter syndrome, but I did feel like everything was—I feel like everything *is*—constantly on the verge of crashing down, including myself.

I've been told I'm resilient, but being in survival mode for over a decade has been beyond exhausting. I've often thought of what I'd have to do if I had to start all over. What would it be like to find myself in a job market where systemic ageism, sexism, and racism are buried in the foundations of almost every institution?

It's frightening.

"Frightening" may not be the most accurate word to use here, as I am not scared to do things alone, and I am no stranger to hard work. I usually face my fears and have discovered my own courage.

A more precise term might be "disheartening."

My heart has often been my guide, ever since my paternal grandfather showed me generosity of spirit.

In my twenties, my first boyfriend was the love of my life. He taught me how to trust, how to communicate, and how to be vulnerable. It didn't matter if we were separated by several states or entire continents.

I am forever grateful for the love this first boyfriend provided.

Since then, I have never been as close romantically to other men in my life—not even when I was, as happened twice, engaged to them.

After I realized the second engagement would not work, I faced being alone for the first time in my adult life. Before 2010, I had never been out of a relationship for more than a month at a time.

Since 2010, I've dated fewer than half a dozen men, and usually for about three-month stretches.

As a friend said, "Dating after thirty is like thrifting. It's a lot of sorting through garbage in the hopes that you'll find a buried treasure someone else stupidly threw out."

Mobile apps have facilitated toxic environments; they are rife with fraud and lies.

As a consequence, my romantic life has been unsteady. I'm looking for a partner, not an inadequate roommate. While I choose to be alone rather than suffer an inappropriate boyfriend, I nevertheless still hope for the proverbial "someone special."

Am I a statistic in the loneliness epidemic that few want to acknowledge? I'm not close to my remaining family, and my friends (though wonderful) don't quite satisfy the daily emotional quotient I need.

My steadiest companion has been curiosity, which keeps me from falling into despair. I am eager to find out what happens next, how something works, why things are the way they are. Curiosity retains the power to rejuvenate me and give me joy. I come alive when learning about a new topic; I feel my senses awaken, stimulated by discovery and novelty.

But I'll confess that when, a little before midnight, I must close the book, turn off the television, put down the internet, I tense up with the awareness that I'll soon be alone, once again, before sleep.

With one click of the lamp, I return to darkness.

In the dark, I am almost instantaneously back on that tightrope. Slowly, but endlessly, I am crossing the chasm, heading toward the abyss. The roar of my thoughts competes with people rooting for me to fail. They cheer any misstep: real, perceived, or concocted.

But I cannot stop. This is my destiny. My lot in life. So I keep walking, like Gatsby ran toward the green light with his arms outstretched.

One day I will learn if the tightrope becomes a noose or a lifeline. I'm curious to see what happens next.

Black People Don't Do This

ASHALIEGH CARRINGTON

Black people don't do this, Ash. We just don't do this.

What we do is grab a glass of champagne, or wine, or even beer, and drink. We pray it washes away all the memories that keep us awake at night. That's the communion rite every evening at six. It doesn't matter whether it's the bar or the living room, because as long as it leaves a smile, we'll be all right.

If it doesn't work, we'll drive down to the infested corner store and grab a pack of Newports and play some numbers. Family members' birthdays are good luck.

When luck gets low, Uncle Thomas or Aunt Debra explain that there's a real problem and drag us to church. If God's own communion doesn't work, then there's Alcoholics Anonymous or Nicotine Anonymous.

And if AA and NA and every other group with an "A" fails, nobody can say effort wasn't made. No blame.

But Ash, you've never wanted to do that. You were turned off by both drinking and smoking before anyone could turn you on to either one.

You never sought out weed, because all weed did was remind you of the child-support parking lot, a small brick building with Black bodies flowing in and out.

What's there to cling to when you can't cope with your own trauma? You refused to forget.

Your flirtation with suicide started when you were nineteen. You began staring at the train tracks after every class. On the walk home, Death became your companion, telling you to bend over the bridge that would take you home. Soon enough, she found a way into everything. She sat, dangling her legs next to the medicine cabinet. She twirled on the edges of knives during dinner. She even gilded round and round on the ceiling fan.

She had you sleeping in until three in the afternoon because she kept you up all night. Every time you sat down with your worried mom, you lied, and answered back that you were fine. It was only your mother who convinced you that you needed help. She said you had to stay alive for your cousin's eighth-grade graduation. There was no way that your self-destruction was going to overshadow your little cousin's accomplishment.

So that's how you ended up sitting in a therapist's office looking at *Psychology Today* and *Mental Health Monthly*, wondering why there were no Black people on the cover.

It doesn't help that your therapist is a middle-aged white woman.

Every time you bring up a racist moment in your life, she can't understand it.

There's no medicine, you discover, for microaggressions. All the doctor can say is "I'm sorry" or "How did that make you feel?" If you had a dollar for every time she sat there with her pen in hand and said "I understand" when she had no idea what she was talking about, you could pay for these sessions in cash.

She has a little machine that makes a low sound to drown out other people's conversations while you sit in the waiting room. It's an effective device called "white noise."

Why am I sitting in this room listening to this? It bounces over every corner of the room. I am not asking for her to play Marvin Gaye or Jay-Z, but with all this white noise I can't even hear my own thoughts. Silence would have been fine for me.

And why does she keep the door open? You have to sit in the same corner every visit so no one will see you.

The last thing you need is for someone to tell your grandmother that they saw you in a doctor's office, getting mental help.

Hell, it is more acceptable in our community to smoke weed with your grandfather on a Sunday morning than to be mentally ill.

If a family friend catches you in here, you might as well tell them that you are here because you got PTSD. That way, the rumors across the neighborhood will at least be true: the rumors that nobody brought you up right, the whispers that you—the smart one of your family, the one that was going to take care of everybody—had somehow become crazy.

But what counts as crazy?

I'm smart enough to know I need help. How can Black people tell other Black people: "We don't do this?" Black people are doing this. Hell, last time I checked, I am Black. And I am doing this.

Fierce Women of All Age

DEBORAH HOCHMAN TURVEY

My mother was one of those women who thought there was no problem that couldn't (or shouldn't) be solved by taking a shower and making your bed. A to-do list kind of gal, a pioneer woman if the lower east side in NYC counted as homesteading, she sewed our dresses, knit our sweaters, cooked everything, made wallpaper out of old flour sacks, and retiled the bathroom floors.

All that, a master's degree, four children, and a job while supporting our dad in his quest for a PhD.

Our house was riddled with contradictions. Our mom was the go-to if we needed something done, something lined with shelf paper, a schoolbook wrapped in a brown paper bag, or a situation handled. Our dad was our go-to for emotional support. There were no gender norms in our pink Victorian house filled with four daughters, two dogs, two parents, and, as my dad once said, enough tampons to have purchased a Greek island. Other kids got Barbies for Chanukah (let's face it, most kids had Christmas—a fact that did not get unnoticed), while we got tickets to Broadway shows, a bucket of change to count, and a box with our favorite food—and books, always books.

We were taught by both our parents that our voices mattered (unless we were singing) and that we should make them heard but to please make it interesting. And if it wasn't interesting, at least make it funny.

I remember my dad—who got his PhD in psychology—once telling me that the only thing more boring than the fights I had with my then-boyfriend was having to listen to them.

Lesson learned. It's not the only time he reminded us that people paid him to listen to their problems, so cut the bullshit, keep it short, get to the point, or otherwise be prepared to pay.

There were lots of rules in our house, but most didn't make sense to our friends. Swearing was fine; name-calling was not. Curfews didn't exist. Sharing was optional ("Show me how you share a toy"); taking turns was mandatory. And the very worst thing you could say to someone was "shut up."

That philosophy served me well when my husband and I had kids. We started them off small, and by that I mean, small moments while they were small. We prepared for them little snacks of activism and community. My oldest went to her first march across the Brooklyn Bridge for Planned Parenthood at age three, while the middle one hopped on the train with me at ten months to walk (or be carried) in a Planned Parenthood march in DC. She kept smiling and waving in her Baby Bjorn as "pro-lifers" yelled at her and me, "Why didn't you kill that one?"

I took them out of school to watch Obama get sworn in, to participate in town-wide postcard parties, and to join me, my sisters, and one million other women in DC for the Women's March the day after Trump was elected. After all, my sisters and I had started small too. We got our start singing union-organizing songs while camping across the states in our mustard-yellow VW van—or maybe it was when our dad left for a few weeks to go train volunteers in the Peace Corps? Or maybe it was just in the day-to-day caring for others modeled for us by our own remarkable mother? Whatever it was, it was definitely an all-for-one, one-for-all mentality in our house—more of a commune or kibbutz, where everyone was always welcome and there was enough rosehip tea and homemade yogurt to go around.

Life is not one moment but lots of little moments, like money in the bank, one coin at a time. Some pennies, some nickels, and some golden dollars. It's not the single events that matter; it's all the moments in between. Like a good dinner, you need all the courses, but please don't skip the bread.

And when in doubt, whether it's camping in a VW van or marching across the Brooklyn Bridge, surround yourself with a large, smart group of sisters and friends, or to make your own community wherever you are. Because being fierce, standing up for yourself, speaking out for others, doesn't mean there are no self-doubts, missed opportunities, mistakes made, tears of joy and sadness . . . and it's all so, so much easier when you share . . . or at least take turns.

Our Monikers

HEIDI MASTROGIOVANNI

I graduated from high school in 1975, the year after the Equal Credit Opportunity Act passed. Among other reforms, this law made it possible for women to obtain loans and credit cards in their own name.

My mother was born in 1923, three years after women in the United States finally won the right to vote. My parents had many good qualities. They could be generous and caring. They could also be volatile. My father yelled very loudly when he was angry. When someone upset my mother, she would not speak to or look at the offending party for days. This was terrifying for a young child, and not much fun for a teenager.

When I became engaged to my first husband, keeping my name was such a given for me, I didn't spare it a second thought. At some point before the wedding, I was on the phone with my mother and mentioned that I would not be taking Dennis's name. My mother was instantly furious, which couldn't have been a surprise, since I knew how stridently traditional she was. At that point I was living in New York City and my parents were in Connecticut in our family home, so if she decided to not speak to me, it would hardly affect my day-to-day life. Yet I remember reacting with fear, despite being an adult.

"What does Dennis think about that?" she demanded.

"He's fine about it. Otherwise I wouldn't be marrying him."

Apparently I felt more anger than nervousness, and apparently my tone conveyed that.

My mother changed tactics. She started crying. And I immediately felt guilty. She whimpered that my grandmother (her mother, who had passed away a few years before) would have been so upset to see me doing this. I just wanted my mother to stop crying. I promised I would change my name to honor my grandmother.

Well, my mother was happy, and she hung up the phone and probably continued being happy. I hung up the phone and was furious with her, and even angrier with myself for giving in to that emotional blackmail.

I avoided thinking about what I had promised. Dennis and I got married.

My credit cards and all my documentation went unchanged. The subject of my name didn't come up again between my mother and me. Until a funeral for one of my legion of elderly Italian relatives.

We were at a funeral home in New Jersey. There was a book for people to sign and leave messages of condolence. I automatically wrote "Heidi Mastrogiovanni." Later, I happened to glance at the guestbook and saw written next to my name in my mother's very neat handwriting a hyphen and my husband's last name.

I scanned the room. My mother was talking to my father's sisters. I stomped over, grabbed her by the arm, and pulled her to an empty corner. I was still fiercely livid about being acquiescent the first time. I wasn't going to make that mistake twice.

"I saw what you wrote. Don't ever do that again. Don't change my name. If you do, that will be the last time you see me."

I meant what I said. I watched my mother's reaction. I swear, her face conveyed that she was considering matching my outrage and then decided against it. Instead, she whispered, "But you said you would take Dennis's name to honor my mother."

"Yes, I did. And I shouldn't have. And you shouldn't have tried to make me agree to something I didn't want to do."

Years later, my dear Dennis died. When I married my dear second husband, Tom, six years after, my parents flew to Los Angeles for our wedding. My mother never commented on what my name would be when I got married again. My sense of her silence was that it was not inspired by condemnation. And that shouldn't have been a surprise to me. My mother never let anyone, including my father, boss her around. She had her way of marching with the changes progress brought.

We are all, to some extent, children and warriors of our times. I'm part of the *Our Bodies, Ourselves* generation. I think of now as the *Our Monikers, Ourselves* era: Keep our names, change them, hyphenate them, make our birth names our middle names. Whatever we decide, call us by the names we call ourselves.

What's in a [Last] Name?

NIAMH CUNNINGHAM

September 21, 2015

In a short while I will be getting married and will change my last name. The question of whether I will change my name is usually the second or third question people ask when they find out I'm engaged, right after when is the date and where are we going on our honeymoon. Some people have expressed surprise at my decision; some have expressed admiration; absolutely no one has asked my fiancé, Paul, if he intends to change his name. It is not a question men get when they tell people they are engaged, nor is it a discussion men have over a few beers while watching the game. If they are talking about anything wedding-related at all, it's probably about the bachelor party. Women, on the other hand, will have extensive conversations over bottles of wine discussing their decisions to change or keep their names, and everyone has her own, personal reasons for her decision. My reason is pretty simple—I want to. I want to enter the reception as the new Mr. and Mrs. Emerson. I want Paul and me to be a unit created in matrimony and sealed with vows, and I want the unit to have the same last name. On a very basic level, I want the unit to have the same monogram. Maybe I'm more old-fashioned than I thought, but I have a long list of women who came before me in my family who, when they took their men, took their names.

I didn't always want to change my name. When I was a child, we realized that there was only one boy, my cousin Mark, who could carry on the family name. I remember telling my dad not to worry; I won't change my name, and the name will live on through me. It was an early indication my parents were raising a feminist. Then, when I was thirteen, my cousin Niall Cunningham was born, and with two boys it seemed to absolve the girls of the responsibility. During our engagement, I had a few stretches where I didn't think I wanted to go through with the change. I even came up with what I thought was a reasonable compromise: Paul and I should change both our names to Emerham and start a whole new tribe. I realized that sticking with Cunningham wasn't necessarily a feminist gesture. Cunningham was my dad's name, and it was his dad's name before him, and his dad's name before that. My name is not Marsh or Moran or Snee or Harte, and even those names are patriarchal. But I quickly learned that from a legal standpoint, it is much easier for me to change my name after marriage than it is for Paul to change his name for any reason at all. Society isn't as ready for men to change their names as this generation is.

I have nothing to complain about my new last name, either. It will be the names of our future children if we are blessed enough to have any. Emerson goes well with Niamh (pronounced Neeve—it's Gaelic), and it has three fewer letters than Cunningham—a bonus if I ever have to fill out a Scantron bubble sheet again. It bumps me down the alphabet by two letters, so I will have to get used to that at the voting booths and will-call windows.

I am incredibly proud of my accomplishments as Niamh Cunningham, but I am very much looking forward to my adventure as Niamh Emerson, especially knowing I will have Paul beside me as we make our way. In her memoir, *Auto da Fay*, Fay Weldon writes, "Names are important. . . . With every change of name comes a change in fortune. . . . No change in fortune should be seen as magic, only as a function of altering views of the self." In what will indeed be a magical moment, I will not magically become a different person when the priest pronounces us man and wife. Plus, one thing is pretty clear in my family: You can take the Cunningham out of a girl's name, but you will never take the Cunningham out of the girl.

Fierce Is In

PEGGY TANNER

When I think *fast*, I think of middle school and the girls who outpaced me in the fifty-yard dash. I think of the girls the boys prayed the bottle would land on during a game of spin the bottle. For me, fast is out and *fierce* is in.

My life has been defined by breaking barriers. As a young girl I had no awareness that I was trespassing on male turf, but as I look back, and thanks to my parents' support, I seamlessly crossed into male territory. In elementary school, I was the first girl to be a school crossing guard. During recess, I dominated baseball card trading games and came to possess one of the most coveted baseball card collections. In high school, I was the first female drummer in the high school marching band and the only girl member of the audiovisual squad. At Dartmouth College, my female classmates and I were considered pioneers, transforming an all-male college into a coeducational one. Professionally, I was among a handful of women working in the early 1980s on a Wall Street trading floor navigating misogyny, strippers, and fratty bro behavior. And the list goes on. . . .

My older sister and I were raised to believe we could be whatever we set our minds to. Yes, hard work was required, but without any brothers, my parents never defined us by our birth sex. When I was a child, my parents were unfazed when I preferred G.I. Joe to Barbie; they laughed when, after receiving my first pocketbook, they looked inside and found baseball cards and mascara. They got a kick out of my captaining (some might say, bossing) the boys around in our nightly neighborhood kickball games.

In second grade, for my seventh birthday, I begged my parents for a football uniform. To keep my gift a surprise, my parents suggested that perhaps a ballerina tutu might be more appropriate. I cried, cajoled, and cried some more! On the morning of my birthday, my parents and my sister paraded into my room with a teddy bear dressed in a football uniform. I was ecstatic. For weeks on end, I wore my uniform to school and proceeded to plead with the commissioner of the town's Midget League football to allow me to play. I offered to cut my hair short and do whatever was needed, but his response was an emphatic "no." Instead, he recommended I consider becoming a cheerleader. No offense to any cheerleaders, but I wanted to play with the boys, not cheer for them from the sidelines. Better yet, I dreamed of girls having teams of their own.

In the '60s, the opportunity to play organized team sports for girls was limited, but as I grew older, interscholastic girls' sports teams grew exponentially. Team sports were and continue to be a defining part of my life. The friendships I formed were "forever" friendships, and I treasure those connections. As a member of a team, I learned the importance of working together, communicating with my teammates, and always leaving my ego on the bench. These important life skills have served me well on and off the field.

Being a tomboy in the '60s felt like a privilege and an advantage. I never felt I was born into the wrong body, but instead relished being free to be me. It was easier being fierce when I was not intimidated by the other sex and felt comfortable being outnumbered and, occasionally, bullied on a kickball field, in a college classroom, or working on a trading floor. And it was significantly easier being fierce when supported by strong female friendships.

With phenomenal women by my side, I feel more than fierce; I feel invincible.

State of My Soul

POLLY INGRAHAM

He broached the topic when we were walking along the Charles River one fall evening, with the lights twinkling on the Cambridge side. Our wedding date had been set for the following September. We were holding hands, not speaking of anything much. Then, in came a torpedo.

"I accept that you're not Episcopalian and am not about to try to convert you or anything. But there is something I've been wondering about."

We kept walking, but I braced myself.

"I know you've never had any interest in being baptized, but it would mean a lot to me. The process is not that big a deal, and doing this could bring us closer."

He got it all out in one fell swoop, then, stopping to see my reaction, let go of my hand. The waves were looking choppier now. I felt rebellion bursting out from every pore.

"Closer, how exactly? I thought we were doing fine staying just who we are. I'm learning all I can about your world; isn't that enough?" My body stiffened, my inner core defending itself against assault.

"Yes, yes, I'm not trying to change you; this would just create more of a shared experience between us. Baptism allows you to become one of God's own, always protected." True to him, utterly ridiculous to me.

Still, I realized that *he was actually worried about the state of my soul*. He was standing in a beautiful room with a high ceiling and vases of flowers and colorful pillows and streams of light coming in, a staircase leading up to an even more beautiful top floor.

I, meanwhile, was alone outside, shivering. His eyes showed the tremendous longing that was in his heart, a desire to merge the two most precious parts of his life.

His anxiety, which he was trying to wear lightly, made me want to run. Screw this!

My parents and my grandparents had NOT put me on an exposed cliff to perish.

We were taking up the whole sidewalk now, letting people pass on both sides.

"I've lived all this time as an unbaptized person, and I refuse to accept that I am somehow incomplete. Do you want me as I am, or do you want a false version of me?" I spread my arms out wide, demonstrating that he was calling for my sacrifice. "And why have you not mentioned this until now?"

He didn't answer right away, gazing out at the river where, in the early mornings, he found peace in rowing. Sculling was a solitary activity; preparing for marriage, however, required two people in balance.

A few months later, Boston was reeling from a terrible crime. A pregnant white woman was found murdered after an evening Lamaze class. While a black man came under suspicion and then was taken into custody, eventually, after he jumped to his death, it came to light that her own husband had actually plotted the murder to get a hefty insurance payout.

I had a nightmare after seeing the grainy newspaper pictures of the once smiling couple and then the dark-haired woman sprawled lifeless on the sidewalk. I woke up feeling that I was also being attacked by the man I thought I loved. Everything got flipped to its opposite. The next day, I walked shakily toward the tall, red, airborne sculpture that marked my T stop. Maybe Rob *could* possibly wield his faith like a weapon; maybe I still didn't know him well enough to marry him.

In divulging the nightmare to Rob, I was demanding a resolution. He held his head in his hands and looked as if he'd been punched in the gut. "I hope you know that I would never hurt you," he said. Guiding me to the starting line of Christianity was supposed to be all about enhancing my life, not threatening it.

After this, there was no more talk of baptism. I tried to quell any flickering doubts about both the safety of my soul and the legitimacy of our union amid the thousand clear signs—the fireworks exploding in a rainbow of colors— that our love would go on flourishing.

The dream, though, put me on guard. A part of me had broken away from the dizzy-in-love part and climbed up the mast of the ship he and I were sailing on. It would look out for any vessel that might surreptitiously approach, even in broad daylight, to deliver pirates that would take me prisoner—with my husband's consent.

May the Fierce Be with You

LAURIE LAIDLAW

A clear cool mountain morning in July in Jackson Hole. My happy place—
the one week of every year that I would spend at the ranch sprawled along
the Snake River. With the Tetons as a magnificent backdrop and my horse
underneath, I would ride for hours—through cool forests and cold streams,
across green meadows, then gallop home on dusty trails. A long-anticipated
day—the day I traveled to the ranch—the day I lived.

The indigestion I felt after having lunch at a favorite spot, Moose,
Wyoming, turned into lower back pain later while unpacking at our cabin at
the ranch. During dinner at the ranch house, it worsened. I looked around—
my soon-to-be husband, Jim, and others not in view—so I made what turned
out to be a poor decision and headed back to the cabin alone, leaving
everyone else. An important lesson—low back pain and nausea can mean
internal bleeding. As I bent to take off my cowboy boots, I was hit with the
most excruciating pain imaginable. Drenched in cold sweat, I crawled out to
the porch where I could be seen. No one was around, and no one picked up
their cell. I dialed 9-1-1—this was smart.

The first to find me—and the first of the Fierce—was the woman from the
next cabin. A cancer survivor and a nurse, she began to check my vitals. She
held my hand while the ranch owner (himself a first responder) arrived and
gave me oxygen. I was in shock. I vaguely remember the ambulance arriving
after a long time.

What I do remember clearly is the EMS tech who rode with me in the
ambulance—a fit tan woman with short dark hair and brown eyes. She held
my face in her hands. Looking hard in my eyes, she repeated, fiercely, "Stay
with me . . . stay with me . . ." I was drifting, going then coming back. The
second of the Fierce Ones.

I was in and out of awareness in the ER. After a CT, the attending informed
me and Jim that I had a large mass in my mesentery (or abdomen), which
appeared to be a lymphoma that was bleeding. He suggested airlifting me

to Salt Lake. Unbeknownst to me, the next day a whole new set of Fierce Ones put in motion a plan to have me flown by medical jet to the Cleveland Clinic: my friend Liz; work colleague and benefits VP, Ellen; and sister-in-law in Patient Services, Kathy. By a miracle, the paperwork was done, I was cleared, and the pilots (also Fierce Ones) gunned the jet down the runway to beat the 9:15 p.m. airport deadline for takeoffs. As I left the JH hospital, the nurses and doctors gathered to wish me good luck. How I envied their "normal lives" as the scenario played out in my mind—cancer—I would fight hard; I would lose eventually—I would never see my children married or see their children. I was not Fierce.

Arriving by ambulance at the Cleveland at 2:00 a.m., I am immediately given liters of lifesaving blood. Fierce lesson: Please donate blood if you are able. Miraculously, I am still alive. At the clinic, more Fierce Ones surrounded me and were my advocates. A radiologist and dear friend who immediately became involved—and fiercely staved off the general surgeons—another life-saving act for me. The attending—she never gave up and stayed on my case until the real issue revealed itself. My husband, Jim, who stayed by side and never doubted I would pull through. My vascular surgeon—who found the aneurysm in my mesentery that had burst in Jackson Hole, which was still bleeding and which was luckily being held in check by the blood and fluid that had filled my abdomen or I would have bled out. Standing at the foot of my bed he announced, "I found the problem. And I will fix it." I burst into tears. I looked in his eyes—one of the many Fierce Ones.

I became Fierce at that moment.

What I learned: In a severe medical emergency that we may not survive, our body and our mind protect us from the severity, the pain, and allow us to slip into unconsciousness and death. In my weakened state, I was not able to be Fierce. The key to survival at this point are the Fierce Ones around us—a spouse, family member, nurse, or doctor. Their advocacy for us—insisting "stay with me" when our life is ebbing—is critical.

The Fierce Ones—they surrounded me, protected me, and saved me. So now I know that if a friend, family member, or loved one is in the situation I was, I will be One of the Fierce. For them. May the Fierce be with you and protect you in time of need.

Speak Your Truth

NICOLE DECKER-LAWLER

Like bookends, I began and ended 2020 with miscarriages. Clear Blue Easy tests read "Pregnant," which filled me with elation, only to be quickly replaced by heartbreak. The first miscarriage left me traumatized. I processed my loss by speaking openly with anyone who would listen, from acquaintances to paid professionals. They became my way to cope with this tragic loss. I educated myself and learned these types of mishaps were quite common. One in eight pregnancies ends in this fashion.

The first causality was a painful shock. The second left me broken to the core. My doctor, husband, and I had viewed the ultrasound, which showed an image that resembled a small olive. There was the embryonic sack with a tiny pimento baby wiggling at its center. We heard its fast, strong heartbeat. We were elated! I soon experienced symptoms that prompted a second visit with my physician. The exam showed my little one had stopped developing a few weeks prior. A D&C was scheduled, and the baby who never had a chance was extracted from my womb.

I spent days wrapped securely in a duvet. I binge-watched with glassy eyes countless hours of streaming television. I refused to speak with any visitors who called upon our home. I had failed. I failed to create a growing healthy baby for a second time. I failed to conceive a sibling for my then four-year-old son. I failed to generate a larger family for my beloved husband. I was mentally and physically broken. I felt I had let everyone down.

When I felt strong enough to exit my cocoon, I seated myself on a soft chair across from my holistic doctor in a peach-colored room.

In that coral room, with tears running down my face and wearing a white cloth mask that closely resembled a jockstrap, my specialist probed me with questions on how I was doing with the losses, the pandemic, and life in general.

"I don't want to be pregnant."

That simple comment freed me of my enslavement to my own unmet expectations, the desires of my family, and any unrealistic assumptions mandated by society. Not everyone is meant to adapt to the house in the suburbs, white picket fence with 2.5 kids life.

I realized that I no longer wanted to continue fighting this battle. I couldn't endure another baby bereavement. I no longer desired to explore any further treatment options such as medications, procedures, or therapies to statistically increase my probability of conceiving. These only inflated my risk of additional mourning. This was no longer worth it to me.

I was thankful for being the biological parent to one amazing kid. He was happy, healthy, and everything a parent could want in a child. My little man was thoughtful, kind, energetic, and had a zest for life. He has taught me to appreciate what I have and not always pine for something I am lacking. As a mother, I didn't need quantity. I already had quality.

The late Supreme Court Justice Ruth Bader Ginsburg once stated, "It's a woman's right to control her own destiny, to be able to make choices without the Big Brother state telling her what she can and cannot do." By saying "I don't want to be pregnant" out loud, I manifested my own reproductive fate. Those simple words untethered me from a concept of maternity that no longer suited me. I freed myself from the complications of calamitous conceptions and granted myself the permission to let it all go.

Battle of the Pregnancy Bulge

SHERRY PINAMONTI

I never gave much thought to the process of becoming a mother. I knew the perfunctory mechanics that I learned in health class. I lived under the assumption that a penis would get me pregnant with 100 percent accuracy and it was my job to deflect these inevitable babies with contraception like Wonder Woman bouncing sperm off her magic bracelets. *Pew! Pew!* Then, when the time was right, I would take off my magic bracelets and become a mother nine months later.

My first pregnancy, I naively announced to everyone that I was pregnant as soon as I found out. Several weeks later, with tears welling in my eyes, I retracted my joy in increments of "I lost the baby" statements. My miscarriage made me feel betrayed by my body. This caused a methodical self-interrogation, like an MRI machine repetitively clanking, over every decision I had made up until that point.

After a smooth pregnancy and healthy baby, I assured myself that the first miscarriage was a systems check and my body had worked out the kinks. After all, I had been the owner of a menstruation assembly line for two decades with a womb that bragged, "It's been 7,300 days without baby!" A sudden major production change, like Ford's assembly line being repurposed to build B-24 bombers in WWII, was bound to cause confusion during the first run. However, one perfect crying and pooping prototype didn't guarantee more. I had three more miscarriages in a row.

I wasn't the campy 1970s television Wonder Woman from three paragraphs ago. I was gritty, battle-hardened, World War II Wonder Woman from the comic books.

Pregnancy for me was asymmetrical warfare, and I was playing every role in my battle of the pregnancy bulge. I was the soldier seeing the bloody losses; the steadied general sending in wave after wave of troops; the sweetheart gazing at a black-and-white ultrasound photograph; the death notification officer informing my husband of another loss; the POW keeping faith.

I woke to warm, sticky lost battles, and even publicly lost a battle while pumping gas on Christmas Eve. I'd flush and bury my causalities, and pray this was the last time. Occasionally, overly curious people would ask me when I was going to give my child a sibling. I'd act coy and say, "I don't know" or "We'll see." Nosy people become adamant when they think you're holding out on having children. So I told a pushy person that I was currently miscarrying. That conversation ended abruptly. I felt a release that emboldened me to tell more people.

I quickly realized that many people don't know how to be supportive of something they can't fix, and they only have a finite amount of support to offer when it's a situation they wouldn't entertain. I certainly didn't picture myself with five miscarriages under my belt, and by belt I mean my above-the-waist elastic-banded maternity leggings. But there I was. I could see people's eyebrows arch as they calculated my losses in column A versus the win in column B. To some my story was a Pyrrhic victory; to me it was just how I built my family. I began selling emotional war bonds to reinforce that those around me remained invested in and supportive of my objective. For every "Maybe it's a sign," "Maybe you should take a break," or "You're crazy," I'd gently smile and assure everyone I was fine, collect their emotional capital, and promise playdates, cousins, and grandkids down the road.

I was caught in a miscarriage Catch-22. Society said I could stop trying to have babies whenever I wanted. All I had to do was start openly discussing my miscarriages. The caveat was that society didn't condone the discussion of miscarriages. Years later, I no longer fly pregnancy missions, but like an old veteran that doesn't care what you think, I talk freely about my miscarriages. It is my sincerest hope that no woman should have to be both the USO and the soldier in her pregnancy battle.

The highest awards in the military are bestowed on soldiers who, if they told you in the moment what they were going to do and sacrifice, the overwhelming response from the public would be, "You're crazy." Today the bracelet that jingles as I write has three medals with each of my children's names on them.

A Poem to Miss Carriage on the Occasion of Lockdown

HANNAH BALLOU

I'm three days into my pandemic miscarriage. Day 1: Cry. Bleed. Repeat. Day 2 is devoted to drinking wine and getting camera-fucked by a sonographer who told me what I already know; no heartbeat. No good. Our minuscule erstwhile family member made its grand debut onto my toilet paper. I took a photo of it, but no filter in the world is making that thing Instagrammable.

The dashed hopes of miscarriage are a very specific breed. My own experience of them is relatively limited so far. Some people face years of them. I'll resist the temptation to quantify and compare misery, but to paraphrase the great Coolio, ain't no miscarriage like a lockdown miscarriage, 'cause a lockdown miscarriage is even lonelier.

A Poem for Miss Carriage on the Occasion of Lockdown

Excuse me, Miss, you seem to have left
A red stain in my pants.

I'm thirty-nine; that might have been
My final bloody chance.

I squinted at those pregnancy tests
And finally saw a line.

I suffered through the family Zooms
Without a bottle of wine.

Lockdown canceled theater,
Which caused me lots of pain.

"But at least," I told myself,
"I'll make a tiny brain."

Journalists predicted
A lockdown baby boom.

But my little "Quarenboomer"
Is trickling out my womb.

Your uninvited visit left my cha-cha
Cramped and dribbling.

YOU can break it to my daughter
She won't have a sibling.

I am not a rich woman, Miss.
I do not have a trust fund.

No cash for IVF, alas.
I have to fuck my husband.

"Once more unto the breach, my love.
I cannot fight this urge.

You're hotter than Jon Hamm, my love.
(When luteinizing hormones surge.)

I'm joking, Darling,
Come back here and give a girl a hand;

Deliver the goods then fall asleep,
While I do a shoulder stand."

Preggers at forty isn't a breeze.
It takes hard work and luck.

So, Miss Carriage, next time around,
Off you fucking fuck!

Bread and Rocks

LINDSEY KEEFE

It's a perfectly average morning on maternity leave: I'm propped up in bed, feeding the baby, and with my free hand I'm typing into Google the question I ask it daily—"How can I tell if I'm depressed or if my life just sucks?"

I had been depressed once before while in graduate school, a months-long episode that culminated in fantasies about climbing from my bathroom window onto the roof and walking until I met the asphalt three stories below. I'd pace my attic apartment and obsess about *Jane Eyre*.

My God, I'd think, *Bertha Rochester must've been a graduate student!* Most tragically of all, it didn't occur to me that this deeply earnest revelation was at least a tiny bit funny.

This feels different. I don't want to hurt myself, and anyway, our bathroom window is ninety years old and won't open more than a crack. I'm madly in love with this new baby with her quick, gummy smile and her chatty, sweet big brother, but still I write in my journal every day, "I feel like I'm trapped under something heavy." I suspect the real problem is that my lack of appreciation for my life has somehow made it all go bad. It's horrifying. I tell no one except Google.

Before I can pour over my search results, I hear a loud series of bangs from downstairs. It's a hollow sound, not like a hammer or a pounding fist, but it's frantic and getting closer. It's coming for us.

I hurriedly put the baby down in the center of the bed and fling the pillows to the floor, guiltily aware that, though we're about to be ax-murdered, the detail about leaving her unattended on a high surface will not go unnoted in the news stories about our deaths.

I creep into the hall, and suddenly my cat, Louie, flies past with something stuck to his front paw. My first, entirely rational thought for this indoor cat in suburban Connecticut is "BEAR TRAP!" and I'm actually close. It's a mousetrap from the recesses of the basement, a plastic rectangle with a pad of glue in the center. The thing is so enormous, it could catch every mouse in the tri-state area—if Pangaea was jammed back together, state lines were redrawn, and now every landmass on the planet officially constitutes the tri-state area.

I chase Louie down, scoop him up like an errant, terrified football, and dash into the bathroom. He's frantic, I'm shaking, and the baby is shrieking with indignation. As I try to pull the trap off, thick globs of glue fly everywhere, but the trap holds tight. We're both covered in glue, the bathroom is covered in glue, and the baby's still screaming. Tufts of white cat hair stick to my glue-covered hands, so now I'm both sticky and slippery, and Louie's head-butting the door. Soap only spreads the glue around, and the cat is alternately getting stuck to the tile floor and gnawing his own foot off, and the baby has stopped wailing, which probably means she's dead—no, wait, there she goes again. I try nail polish remover on my hands and it doesn't work, and the baby's still screaming, and I'm wondering, too late, about toxic chemicals in the glue.

I run downstairs for the industrial-size jug of olive oil and drag it upstairs with me. It works! Louie is free, but also oiled up like he's ready for his debut on the Jersey Shore, or the WWE, or a very specific sort of porn. When he bolts from the bathroom, off to express his displeasure through the subtle art of barfing on things too large or delicate for the washing machine, he leaves greasy footprints in his wake.

And I think, *Is this a metaphor? Is it rock bottom?* And then I think, *Rock bottom is a little bit hilarious.*

I return to the baby, and though I've scrubbed my hands raw, they still have an oily residue. The baby in my arms, already dimply and now well-oiled, is only a sprinkling of rosemary away from being focaccia.

When she's asleep, I reach for my phone again, but not for Google this time. I open my email and start recounting the morning's excitement. It's not a confession, not a distress call, but it's a beginning. If I'm trapped beneath something heavy, maybe I can create the tiniest of wedges in 11-point font and skate free on a slick of olive oil.

Mom and the Night Visitors

MEG SOMMERFELD

I walked down the stairs carrying an overflowing bin of laundry, absentmindedly ticking through my mental to-do list. And then I shrieked at the top of my lungs.

Sitting on top of my dryer was a large, now startled, raccoon. I tried to process what I was seeing (huh-is-that-a-stuffed-animal-no-wait-that-is-that-a-live-racoon-walking-on-the-dryer-OHMYGOD-HOLY$%6#!!) until instinct kicked in and I slammed the door shut as if fending off a horde of Vikings. "There's a raccoon in the basement!" I yelled as my teenage daughter came running. "There's a WHAT . . . ?" she gasped.

With Abby perched behind me, I cracked the door open. The raccoon was still there, but only its legs and hindquarters were visible; it had clambered into the unfinished ceiling and was dangling like a gymnast from the pipes. There it remained for a solid minute, halfway in, half out, apparently using toddler logic that if it can't see you, you can't see it. "You're not invisible, dude, GET OUT!" I yelled, as if it would care.

While "raccoon" might bring to mind cute Disney animals, when one is inside your house, visions of sharp claws, teeth, or rabies tend to eclipse the cuteness. I also felt as if the universe was taunting me to see how much I could take.

The Great Raccoon Visit of 2019 was coming on the heels of a recent divorce, the death of both my parents, a thyroid cancer diagnosis, and a few other curveballs life had thrown my way. This latest debacle felt like the icing on a giant, un-tasty cake of stress.

I didn't know whether to laugh or cry, so I opted for both. In the past, I would have strategized with my then-husband about what to do, or phoned my mom and dad for advice. But now I was on my own, the sole adult in charge.

For the past year, everything seemed to break on cue, as if part of a secret plot: The dishwasher died, a bathroom pipe leaked, and the smoke alarms failed one by one, an abrupt aria of chirps taunting that yet another had gone kaput. Ants invaded the bathroom, and wasps built a nest right next to the front door—not once but twice, just for good measure.

I just could not deal with yet ANOTHER thing breaking; going wrong; needing to be fixed, managed, or handled. But there was no other option. In these moments, I would try to channel my mom's unique blend of stoicism, resilience, and optimism. She would praise my brother or me when we exhibited "stick-to-itiveness" as children, reminding us what a virtue it was to not give up, to see something through to the end, to always try your hardest. Her combination of gentle prodding and encouragement cultivated one of my natural strengths over the years: being diligent and persevering.

And so it was with the raccoon. After the initial shock passed, I took a deep breath and tried to psych myself up. "You are a Girl Scout leader who has taught kids how to kayak and start fires," I reminded myself. "You can handle this." Somehow I kickstarted into problem-solving gear. I called the city's Animal Control office, and when that failed, I Googled and Yelped my way through many listings until I eventually located a service that would remove raccoons. They set a trap, caught him the next day, and blocked up the small hole under the deck where he had squeezed in.

A few days later, a friend texted. "The animals are there to help you," she wrote. "I'm serious; somehow this raccoon was a good thing. I can't tell you how, but keep your eyes and mind open, and you will find the key." She reminded me how in myths, raccoons are undaunted problem solvers who offer lessons in curiosity, adaptability, and resourcefulness. "Maybe the raccoon was your furry little teacher?" Her lighthearted words helped me consider the situation with fresh perspective.

Since then, I've confronted and overcome a variety of challenges. Sometimes in these vexing moments, I crank up an upbeat song in my car and sing along. Sometimes I picture myself like the *Chariots of Fire* runners striding on the beach, my own personal Vangelis anthem playing in my head. I remind myself that every day offers new lessons, some in unexpected places. Although I hope Rocky Raccoon is gone for good, I welcome the reminder to seek out new angles to solve problems—and appreciate the hidden value of unexpected guests.

Breaking Out of the Blue Box

JENNIFER FORREST

From the age of sixteen, I grew up in the Blue Box. My first job was at the global clothing retailer, and I entered the workforce hungry to learn and excited to get a discount on all my new clothes. While there, I was able to implement many of my Nana's treasured words of wisdom along the way, like "Always hold your head up high" and "Beauty is pain, so wear the cute shoes for you, never for someone else." During the next twenty years, while I scaled the walls of the Box, I met my husband, had three sons, and learned many valuable lessons. The toughest one came at the end.

Now in my late thirties, I am proud of my loyalty to this company and the legacy I built there, especially when I had the privilege of helping shape others both personally and professionally. However, right before the pandemic hit, I left the company in search of a new dream. One that provided better work-life balance, a chance to challenge myself, and, let's face it, less folding. It was a leap of faith that I would land on my feet if I took the time to dig deep and trust myself. As COVID-19 spread, leaving the Box was a blessing in disguise. My husband and I decided I would stay home to support our children in virtual learning and, not to mention, handle all the cleaning. So much disinfecting. I began thinking Clorox was a new candle scent.

Fast-forward a year, and I was starting to crave the time to figure out what I was going to do next. I love my boys, but it was time to dream bigger, and I know I am a better mom when I have something that fulfills and enriches my sense of self. I needed to take off the sweatpants and dig the cute shoes out of the closet. I had to listen to that inner voice saying the opportunity is out there.

While contemplating what was next, the Blue Box knocked on the door, asking if I wanted to interview for an available role. I hesitated, but I was also intrigued, as it was a different position than what I had held. Would this role challenge me? Would it get me closer to the goal I had been striving for at the top of the Box?

Two interesting things happened during the interview process. First, in speaking to my potential new boss, he stated, "So you took a year off?" Yes, if that's what you call it. Homeschooling a preteen and a set of twins during a pandemic while balancing their fears for the future is a vacation. All that was missing was the cabana boy with a drink in hand. Second, I learned that the value the company placed on the role was not as significant as my prior roles. The position would not offer the compensation or the growth opportunity I was yearning for. So while I appreciated the opportunity, I politely and timely let them know that it wasn't for me.

The company's reaction was not at all what I had expected. They were angry, livid even. They said I owed them a further explanation. No one in the Box could understand why I turned the job down. Their words, not mine.

Reflecting on the interview process and my years of employment there, I came to the realization that while I was loyal to the company and to the hundreds of amazing employees I led over the years, the Blue Box wasn't always loyal to me. At times, empty promises had shaped and limited my career, and now, again, they had offered me a role without growth opportunities and valued me below my worth. This realization was an awakening.

The power of the Blue Box could have silenced me and my belief in myself. It would have squelched the sixteen-year-old girl. But do you know what? This thirtysomething knows her worth, and I am not afraid to stand up and demand it. I can listen to my Nana's wisdom and hold my head high. The box no longer contains or defines me. I don't owe anyone an explanation but myself. My voice is the one that matters, and I have a lot to say. Plus, I have the cute shoes for the journey ahead.

I'm a Jewish Girl from Brooklyn, and My Story Is About Nuns

RHEA HIRSHMAN

You might think that, as a Jewish person growing up in a predominantly Jewish Brooklyn neighborhood, I would have minimal acquaintance with women in religious orders. You would be partially correct. Although later on, my fascination with comparative religion and medieval history led me to learning a great deal about women religious, in my earliest years my only information about nuns came via my mother through my bubbe (maternal grandmother). Bubbe advised the family that grabbing a button on our clothing when a nun walked by would yield us a surprise. While my grandmother seemed to be the only person to whom the ritual of the button had ever been revealed, my mother transmitted this bit of folk wisdom, to which I faithfully adhered for some years.

Then I started hanging out with Sister Frances Raphael.

That interfaith adventure began when my classmates Jo (Josephine) and Anna Rose, good Catholics and good friends in junior high school, became concerned for my immortal soul. Having been taught, as was common back then, that I could not hope to enter the pearly gates upon my demise, they devised a plan for me to take guitar lessons from Sr. Frances Raphael. Their hope was that guitar lessons would lead us in other directions and that I would—shall we say—come around, increasing the odds of our hanging out together in the afterlife.

Touched that my friends wanted to spend eternity with me and, of course, curious, I accompanied them to the Church of the Good Shepherd to meet Sister. The guitar lessons did lead us off in other directions, although not as Jo and Anna Rose had anticipated. I was by far the better guitar player, and after the second or third "lesson," the guitar stayed home. However, I continued my visits to the convent, where Sr. Frances Raphael and I had lengthy philosophical and theological discussions worthy of a Jesuit or a Talmudic scholar. I relished the distinction of being the only ninth grader in my neighborhood to have an elderly Dominican nun as her own personal theological sparring partner.

Fast-forward to my deep involvement in the women's liberation movement, with feminism providing an additional framework for understanding my affinity for women religious: A self-reliant community of women in a patriarchal culture is inherently subversive.

Although convents were not immune to the excesses of the Church, they also functioned as places of resistance. In times when women were thoroughly devalued, nuns and lay sisters performed all the manual, intellectual, and spiritual labor necessary to life. Always, there was the struggle to retain independence. Ritamary Bradley of St. Ambrose University wrote: "The powerful in both civic and church spheres often plundered the paradisal dream. . . . At various points women (in convents) suffered from imposed claustration, ridicule . . . confiscation of goods and property, and enforced revisions of rules and customs. . . . The core of the struggle was about the obedience of women to men."

You could hardly have scripted a more blatant act of resistance to male authority than the letter sent in March 2010 by Sr. Simone Campbell, executive director of NETWORK, to every member of Congress, urging passage of the Affordable Care Act. NETWORK was founded in 1972 by Catholic sisters committed to social justice work, and the fifty-nine leaders who signed the 2010 letter represented over 90 percent of US Catholic nuns. While the US Conference of Catholic Bishops staunchly opposed the legislation, the sisters, who pointed out that it is they who run many of the hospitals and clinics, and who "witness firsthand the impact of our national health care crisis, particularly on women, children and people who are poor," called their support for the legislation "the *real* pro-life stance." Ouch! Many attributed the legislation's passage to the sisters' outspoken support. The bishops and the Vatican were not happy.

But the sisters have not been deterred, and they remain on the move. Literally. Since 2012, as part of their mission, NETWORK's Nuns on the Bus have created an annual bus tour across the United States to advocate for federal policies supporting economic justice, women's rights, environmental justice, immigration reform, and other issues while engaging thousands of social justice activists along the way.

I doubt that "subverting patriarchy" was the sort of surprise that Bubbe envisaged when she explained the ritual of the button. But none of us— maybe especially spirited Jewish feminists—should be surprised at the power of the Sisters to move the world.

The Refugees, the Rabbi, and the Times Square Police

MARISA ELANA JAMES

I met them at a McDonalds near Times Square, surrounded by out-of-towners seeking cheap Broadway tickets and Instagram opportunities. Hernan and Claudia were asylum seekers from El Salvador, connected with an immigrant support organization where I volunteered as a rabbi. Despite their paying thousands of dollars, their lawyer refused to update them or release documentation. Their case hadn't progressed, and they were nervous.

Rabbinical school prepared me for a lot, but not for this. A pastor friend suggested that I Google the lawyer beforehand, and I was glad I'd taken her advice—the second result was an article about his office defrauding asylum seekers, with consequences only for the people who lost thousands of dollars, some of whom were ultimately deported.

Hernan, Claudia, the interpreter, and I huddled on the sidewalk as Hernan explained their history with this lawyer and their fears about their upcoming deadline.

We entered the building's maze of long beige corridors into a waiting room filled with other families, let the receptionist know that we'd arrived, and sat down to wait.

In the lawyer's office about fifteen minutes later, he was initially friendly and curious—it's probably not often that he has women rabbis in rainbow kippahs joining meetings with his clients. Hernan explained that they were seeking a new lawyer. The lawyer asked who I was. "I'm their rabbi," I answered. He smirked, but it was true—I was one of several clergy in the supportive community that Hernan and Claudia were part of. It didn't matter that they were Catholic and I was Jewish. We shared a vision for a future that included respecting the dignity of every individual, and in this moment especially, my presence was meant to remind the lawyer that he was not treating his clients with either.

The lawyer said that he couldn't release files, as they owed him money. Hernan protested, showing the signed agreement and receipts. When I asked why they couldn't have copies, the lawyer smiled condescendingly at me, one corner of his mouth curled, and started to say, "If they owe me money . . ."

A small flower of rage had been slowly blossoming inside me at the way not only Hernan and Claudia were being treated but everyone in the waiting room, everyone in fear for their lives who had put their trust in this man and received only disdain in return.

For the first time, I interrupted. "I'm sorry," I said. "Did you say 'if' they owe you money? Are you not sure? Hernan has receipts; don't you keep records?"

The lawyer's demeanor instantly transformed. "You know what? I don't want you here." He stood up. "You're trespassing. Get out." We stood as he opened the door, yelling, "These people are trespassing. Call the police. I want them out. NOW."

As we left, the interpreter said, loudly, "We're leaving, OK? You asked us to leave, so we're leaving." But he kept yelling, and as I passed the secretary on the phone, she looked almost bored.

We stayed in the hallway, lest the lawyer accuse us of fleeing a crime scene or something equally absurd.

Minutes later, we heard the elevator doors and the crackly static of a walkie-talkie. Two police officers walked into view, one saying, "We're here; I don't see anything . . ." so I waved and said cheerfully, "I think you're here for us." We began explaining but were soon interrupted by the lawyer, angrily yelling at them to arrest us for trespassing.

One officer moved away with the lawyer; one stayed with us. We could hear the lawyer's voice rising in anger, but we calmly reiterated that Hernan and Claudia were his clients, that our presence was by appointment, that when asked, we had immediately left.

The police conferred. The lawyer again demanded that they arrest us. One officer said to him, "Sir, they're not trespassing. This is a hallway, not private property. They left. We're not arresting them." The lawyer's face glowed red as the officer spoke, and he exploded: "They *are* trespassing! They need to leave *now*! And SHE (pointing at me) *isn't even a real woman of God!*" The interpreter whispered to Hernan and Claudia, and as our eyes met, we all suppressed giggles.

One officer asked the lawyer to please step back inside his office; the other turned to Hernan and Claudia. "He's your lawyer?" They sighed and nodded. The officer shook his head. "Yeah, I think you need a new lawyer."

We couldn't have agreed more.

The Sandwich Queen Manifesto

LISA SMITH MOLINARI

About a million years ago, I had a law career.

I also had a briefcase, an office, a secretary, and a view from the twenty-fourth floor. I did research, argued motions, interviewed clients, and attended the firm holiday party. My name was on a brass plate in the lobby.

But then, when I least expected it, something happened.

That something was an incessant, unrelenting thing called life.

Two years after being unexpectedly blindsided by love, I found myself sitting on my active-duty navy husband's bachelor couch in our dumpy military base house, in a state that did not recognize my law license, nursing our new baby while watching Maury Povich interview people who'd been abducted by aliens.

Twenty-six years, eleven moves, and two more babies later, I'm still making sandwiches and cleaning toilets, and the opportunity to revive my law career simply never came.

Along the way, I discovered that housewifery does not provide one with the obvious sense of achievement that traditional careers offer. In fact, the daily drudgery of housework and mothering is completely taken for granted. Housewives don't get bonuses for sparkling floors, pay raises for fresh laundry, or promotions for perfectly steamed green beans.

Thus, I learned that I had to seize my ego boosts where I could get them.

For instance, one morning while packing my son's lunch for school, I was feeling particularly generous. My usual routine was to roll up three slices of deli meat and place them onto two slices of bread with a leaf of lettuce and a slice of Swiss cheese. But my son had been working hard at football practice, so I decided to create a classic Dagwood, with ham, chicken, and roast beef, two slices of pepper jack, and extra lettuce. It was so thick that I had to pack it into a quart-size storage bag.

On our way home from football practice that afternoon, my son, who was firmly entrenched in that infuriating stage of teenagedom characterized by an almost complete lack of intelligible conversation, said, "Hey, Mom, that sandwich was good."

My heart nearly skipped a beat.

Over the next couple of weeks, I continued crafting thick, meaty sandwiches, sometimes substituting cheeses, adding spicy slices of pepperoni, or a fresh sub roll. Instead of waiting for accolades, I'd taken to eagerly asking him how he liked the sandwich on our ride home from football practice. He would answer in typical teenage brevity, but always communicated appreciation.

Then one day, my son told me that his football buddy said he wished his mom made sandwiches like that. I couldn't believe my ears.

On another exhilarating ride home, I gasped audibly when my son said the school security guard noticed how thick his sandwich was.

I nearly swerved into a ditch the afternoon when he relayed that his coach called him over during practice and said, "Hey, I heard your mother makes you a big deli sandwich every day for lunch. So when are you going to bring one in for me?"

Bolstered by a new sense of culinary superiority, I continued on as a housewife and master sandwich maker for many years with great pride. I took no shame in fishing for compliments where needed, and I commanded respect for those natural nurturers, like myself, who are highly skilled in the domestic arts.

It's true. The closest thing I have to an office has a washer and dryer in it. My briefcase is a Stop 'n Shop bag. And even though my name no longer appears on a brass plate in a lobby, I was the one my kids called when they needed a tissue, help with their homework, a snack, someone to hear about their day at school, or a hug.

While I never made senior partner of a law firm as I'd planned thirty years ago, I attained a status I'd never expected. I became Head Nurse, Accountant, General Manager, Commander in Chief of the House, and, by self-decree, The Sandwich Queen. My scepter may be a toilet bowl brush and my carriage a minivan, but I don't mind, because I am loved by my people.

Genealogy and the Anatomy of an Heirloom

EMILY PARROW

The historical discipline is both a science and an art. I first discovered this in graduate school when my professor assigned a genealogy project. It swallowed me whole. I spent hours ruining my eyesight with digitized census and military records, ship manifests, birth and death certificates, and newspapers.

On one hand, dates, names, and facts have a fixed, detached, and almost clinical quality. But there is a lushness to the study too. I majored in history because its foundation is a mosaic of human stories. Genealogy has a way of teasing empathy from historical research, which, I suppose, was the point of the assignment.

I found that mine was a family of navigators, soldiers, factory workers—immigrants nearly all. At first, it was easy to divorce blunt historical facts from the sentimentality of their belonging to my living, breathing bloodline. Take, for example, one entry:

Daniel Parrow—Originally "Perreault," misheard by some record-keeper—*Born 1876 in Quebec. Railroad Worker and Factory Laborer. Married Genevieve Felio. Six children. Died 1953, possibly in Vermont.*

So it went for a few more generations, but as I continued to decipher sloping handwriting and wobbly typescript, I eventually collided with more familiar names.

Betty, Patty, Ginny.

My great-grandmother and grandmothers, respectively. Three women distant enough to mythologize but possible to materialize. Though they were all gone by the time I turned fourteen, I still remember how it felt to clasp their hands, to be wound in their embraces. As I grafted secondhand stories and fragments of their personalities onto the gaps in indifferent census records, I was struck with how my memories overlapped with only miniscule portions of their lives. It made me miss them more.

I pictured them young, in cities fringed by rivers and punctuated by factories with glossy windows, and in stone-walled towns where church steeples needled the sky. I pictured them on sidewalks and in bright kitchens, soundtrack courtesy of The Cleftones and Glen Campbell.

Shades of ferocity both surrounded and existed within these three women. Sometimes ferocity means viciousness. Inevitably, I transferred these imagined snatches of their lives against the wider shock of the twentieth century, with all its growing pains and presuppositions. All three were grounded (in some cases, one might argue, bound) by religion and family and instilled with the ideas that depression is a construct for self-pitying atheists ("ye of little faith"), a woman's place is in the home, and there is a mere fine line between belonging and ownership.

I wondered if Ginny's parents sang old songs from Italy. After her mother's death, did her father—a veteran of one of the bloodiest American engagements of World War I—bury or resurrect them? He drank himself to death in 1956, and eighteen-year-old Ginny was married thirteen months later. During my research, I found a high school photograph of her on the cheerleading squad. The normalcy of it both shocked and enchanted me.

Sometimes ferocity means tenacity. As a ward of the state, Betty shouldered the burden of rootlessness. The 1930 census lists her mother as an inmate of the Tewksbury State Hospital, and I lost her father's paper trail around the same time.

Patty was born during her mother Betty's first marriage, a brief, searing wound that inspired Patty's (inherited) appreciation for security. She married and settled into the predictable drone of suburban living. A phone call on her fiftieth birthday, heard one-sided by my mother, upset the routine. It was her biological father on the other end.

"I know who you are," Patty said. Her voice was firm, and she didn't thank him for the well wishes. "Please do not contact me again."

Sometimes ferocity implies perseverance. In a photo taken at her second wedding, Betty wears a long-sleeved dress with a velvety sheen and a spray of flowers against the narrow slope of her left shoulder. From that day on, her eyes never lost their starry contentment, that unshakeable joy. I remember her smile best, just as vividly as I remember Ginny's laugh and Patty singing.

For objectivity's sake, I tried to edge history's dual personalities toward a more balanced détente. *You are romanticizing—practically canonizing—these women's lives*, I thought to myself as I clicked my way down a rabbit hole. *Too much, not enough.* But I felt better connected to them that way. Is ferocity inborn or created? As I turned in the finished assignment, I wasn't sure, but I hoped it was an heirloom.

I Broke Up with My Family Over Facebook

JENNIFER RIZZO

My dad passed away in 2014, a few weeks before my first child was born. I still remember finding out he was in the hospital. It was 6:00 a.m. when my alarm went off, and I noticed several missed text messages from my mom.

12:15 a.m.: Your father is having trouble breathing.

1:15 a.m.: He says his chest is tight.

4:00 a.m.: If he doesn't get any better we might need to go to the ER.

5:00 a.m.: He is wheezing and very sleepy. He can't breathe. We're heading to the ER now.

I jumped out of bed, grabbed some pregnancy pants, and threw on unlaced sneakers. I told my husband that my father was in the hospital. As hectic as the moment felt, I can't say it was a surprise. As a result of the childhood trauma that my father never dealt with, he self-medicated with alcohol (Southern Comfort and Heineken were his daily meditations of choice). But none of us ever acknowledged reality. We never talked about my dad's drinking problem. We never talked about enabling his addiction. If something could hurt my family's image, we ignored it.

At the hospital, my two sisters, my brother, and I tried to console my mom. We knew that his liver was the issue and joked about who would be donating part of theirs. But none of us realized the seriousness of the problem until the doctor asked to speak with all of us.

"This can't be a surprise," The doctor said. "All of his organs are shutting down. I'm surprised he has lived this long." The humor evaporated in front of us as I sank to the ground against the wall. I remember thinking that I should tell the rest of the family that we were in the hospital and my dad would be gone in a few hours.

Fast-forward to 2016, the election of Donald Trump, and some of those relatives revealing their true colors.

"If black people didn't resist, they wouldn't be killed."

"Affirmative action is why my child didn't get accepted to his first-choice college."

"Being gay is wrong."

"My kids didn't even know that your dad was black."

This is what my family finally felt comfortable saying now that they thought the man in the White House felt the same way. And for a while, I was silent.

I shut my eyes when they said they didn't see color. I shut my eyes when they joked by calling each other retards and fags. I shut my eyes when they said Trump might be racist but that he is a good president (as if those two things weren't mutually exclusive).

Well, I am not going to shut my eyes anymore.

If my son or daughter is gay, I do not want anyone, including a family member, telling him or her it is wrong. If a cop shoots a person of color, I do not want anyone, including a family member, assuming it had to be justified.

If my family asks why I feel this way, I am happy to share the time my dad was pulled over by police because he was driving his mother's car with a white woman—my mom. Or the time I had to go to therapy because of something "guys just do" because "boys will be boys," even though many of my family members believe that only those who are crazy go to therapy. Or the time my two-, four-, and seven-year-old nephews had to be introduced to their new neighbors because they have dark skin and didn't want someone to call the police when they were seen riding their bikes down the sidewalk in their own neighborhood.

Sometimes those family members say they will contact me, saying they want to stay close. Their "MAGA2024!" post on Facebook page says otherwise, though. Now, I understand all families have disagreements, especially when it comes to politics. But my daughter's wardrobe should not be seen as a political statement, especially since her closet consists of shirts with Sesame Street characters saying "Love has no colors," dresses that state "Call Me President, Not Princess," and sweaters proclaiming "Black Lives Matter."

The truth is, it shouldn't have to happen to you for it to matter to you. I am going to raise my children to be fierce in their love, empathy, and kindness. Ignoring hate, intolerance, and bigotry is not enough, and I refuse to play nice with someone who does not share those same values.

The Night I Made Them Squirm

EMILY TOTH

I'm descended from righteous misfits. My Russian grandfather once ran afoul of the czar—and got sent to Siberia. My parents met at a party for the Communist Party—and immediately campaigned to keep capitalist crooners off the jukebox.

I was five when my mom and her comrades put together a protest. Our local traffic light changed too fast for women and children—so Mom invited the media to our guerrilla theater skit: "Watch us confront New York traffic!"

I played a child. We held hands and crossed the street. I was scared. But we won.

That was my first taste of "demonstrator's high"—the joyous surge of anger when you make the world a better place.

Later, I sat in at segregated movie theaters and marched against the Vietnam War. I supported student strikes and women's right to choose.

I'm still thrilled when I can annoy the hell out of powerful people who are wrong.

This is the story of one of my smallest battles.

• • •

I'd kicked my way through grad school, gotten a PhD, and was teaching at Penn State, living in a sleepy college town.

The locals were average Americans. They voted Republican. They registered for the draft. They were very conservative about what women and men could do.

They did not club together. The women had quilting groups and book clubs. My husband joined a carpentry group but wasn't invited to the men's lodges: Lions, Kiwanis—the pillars of the business community.

But then, nationally, there arose a furor about all-male business clubs.

And one night when I was idly listening to a local talk show . . .

• • •

The young host, "Brett," told us about a local lodge's new scholarship contest, open to all young men! Interested fellows could go to meetings of the "Nittany Club" (I'll call it).

He also invited everyone in his listening audience to call in and comment on anything.

I dialed.

"Is it true," I asked Brett, "that the Nittany Club doesn't admit women because the members are all gay men?"

The phones started ringing.

Brett said he was sure that wasn't true. He blithered and stuttered.

A woman called in. "My husband is a member of the Nittany Club, and he is not a homosexual. I am very sure of that."

A male caller said he was program chair at the Nittany Club. He wanted to reassure "the lady"—me—that the club wasn't involved with homosexuality.

He also offered to send the lady the latest meeting's agenda so she could see that it wasn't about—that thing.

But then he muttered, to my astonishment: "Of course, that lady could just think we left something off the agenda."

Brett switched to another caller.

•   •   •

No conclusions were reached. The program ended with Brett still blithering. No one ever mentioned hearing the show or recognizing my voice. My cats, my husband, and the outraged callers may be the only people who ever heard it.

Still, I call the story a parable, showing how one person with courage and a smart mouth can create social change.

Within a few months, all the men's clubs in our area had opened their memberships to women.

This meant that businesswomen could network with men, and female assistants could meet better bosses. Aspiring women politicians could learn about campaigning. Women could find out how underpaid they were. They could compare notes on sexual harassment.

And the men did have to give up some of their silliness. My professor friend (a traitor to his gender) had been a guest at an Elks meeting where he watched their opening ritual: a prayer to the Great Elk in the sky.

He tried not to "piss myself laughing," he told me. But he had figured out why the clubs didn't want women.

The men in the club weren't being sexual. They were being idiotic.

And they didn't want to be caught in the act.

• • •

O, the political causes I've championed. I can brag—and do—about what we boomers have done to change the world. I've long since moved from Pennsylvania to Louisiana, where people love to hear about Yankee weirdness. "The night I drove Pennsylvania radio down" can make a great song.

I'm not through with asking impertinent questions. If you want people to do the right thing, sometimes you just need to give them a little dose of embarrassment.

I do it well.

Breathe

JENNIFER SAGER

"Jennifer, I want to make sure you understand," he said slowly, gently.

The walls move closer, seem to lurch in my direction suddenly. Is this what they mean when they say the walls cave in around you? I can hardly think. I need a piece of paper to write this down.

"Dr. Ahmed, can you tell me again?"

"Absolutely. Your biopsy results came in. They are highly suspicious for papillary thyroid cancer. We don't know if the cancer is contained to your thyroid or if it is in your lymph nodes. We can't know that until we take out your thyroid and see what's going on. We need to move quickly. I have referred you to an excellent surgeon who specializes in thyroidectomies. You're going to be OK, and I am going to be here every step of the way."

He sounds calm. That's good. But wait, he said cancer? I have cancer. I'm thirty-three; I have a three-year-old and a nine-month-old. I have two small children AND cancer. Cancer. CANCER! CAAAAANNNNNCCCCCEEERRRR!! Oh my God, I'm at work. I've got to get off this phone. I've got to get out of here. Breathe.

"Dr. Ahmed, what comes next? I'm a little overwhelmed." I need to write this down. I need to not say the word "cancer" out loud. There are a dozen people who can hear me right now, sitting just on the other side of this cube wall. Why do we even call them walls when they don't block sound or reach the ceiling? I can't have this conversation here. I can't have this conversation at all. PULL IT TOGETHER, JENNIFER. Breathe. In and out. Again.

"I know this is hard. Do you want to write any of this down so you can share it with Christian later? Take your time. Let me know when you're ready."

"I'm ready. Thank you."

I listen carefully, write it all down, but I can't hang up this phone fast enough. Looking at my notes on the paper all I can see is the word "cancer." CANCER. Tears are welling up in my eyes, clouding my vision, stinging. I've got to leave.

I slam my laptop shut, toss it in my bag with my phone, clutch my keys in my hand, and pause. I take a deep breath in through my nose and let it slip silently out through my mouth. I'm suddenly incredibly grateful for the years of yoga classes that have taught me how to control my breath.

I put my bag on my shoulder. Stand up as tall as I can and make a bee-line for the elevators.

1.

2.

3. . . . I count each step. It gives me something else to focus on.

46 steps. I push the Down button and keep my eyes glued to the doors, praying no one walks by me and tries to make conversation. Praying the elevators are empty. Praying I can make it to my car before I fall apart. Also just . . . praying?

The doors open. I'm alone, but who knows for how long. I press "M" for Mezzanine and ride the ten flights down, relieved each time a new number lights up and the elevator doesn't slow . . . 9, 8, 7, 6 . . . 1.

Finally, the doors open to the lobby and I'm hit with a rush of people. I make my way past them quickly and head for the door to the world.

The hot air feels suffocating, but I keep pushing through. 71 steps. Still counting. Still desperate to get to the privacy of my car. To fall apart on my own terms.

120. I can just see my car. My pace quickens. 140. Almost there. I am practically running now. Tears escaping my eyes, streaming slowly down my cheeks.

165. My hand reaches the passenger door. I hurl myself inside, drop my head in my hands just as the sob I have been holding onto explodes. I fall to pieces as I shut the door, but it's OK. I'm OK. I need this time for me, and I take it.

Breathe. In and out. Over and over and over again. I don't know what comes next, not really. But as the fear and tears wash over me, I know I am going to need to find the strength to figure it out. Because whatever comes next, I need to fight through it my way, and this is the very first step. 1 . . .

The Irrevocable Moments

DANIELLE WARING

As a young college student, learning the value of my voice and my sense of humor while being surrounded by college boys who told me I would be much prettier if I was quieter was quite challenging.

It wasn't until I entered a certain UConn classroom that I truly understood the power of humor. A certain professor first taught me how men and women take up space differently—men sit with their legs spread wide open, expecting everyone around them to make themselves smaller. Women, on the other hand, sit with their legs crossed with their purses on their laps trying to take up as little space as possible. I was once attending a performance in NYC where I watched how the men across from me sat, taking up as much space as possible and forcing everyone else to adjust. I couldn't help but laugh at the accuracy of my professor's description, and I realized I had been seeing this behavior—both literally and metaphorically—for years. Now, whenever I sit next to a man or walk down a hallway, I try to take up as much space as possible and laugh loudly to see what he will do.

The most important lesson I learned in that class, which applies to every single story, play, or script ever written, was that of the "irrevocable moment." She described the "irrevocable moment" as THE moment in a story where once the decision has been made, or action happens, the character can never go back, and will never be the same again.

This moment for me was when I was diagnosed in 2001 with acute myelogenous leukemia. I had just graduated from UConn with my master of arts in Education/English after an exhausting year where I was practically falling asleep in all my classes. I had just accepted a full-time teaching position in Stamford when, after multiple trips to a walk-in clinic, I was rushed to the emergency room and was medically comatose for the next six weeks. While in this coma, I had a stroke, developed sepsis, endured two intravenous rounds of chemo, experienced a tracheostomy (a breathing tube in the windpipe), lost vision in my left eye, and no longer had the ability to walk.

On Sept 11, 2001, as the planes hit the World Trade Center, my family, doctors, and nurses watched the TV in my room with shock, and I was fully cognizant for the first time since arriving at the hospital. As thousands of people prayed for and mourned the lives of family and friends trapped inside, or for the safe return of firefighters or police who were also sacrificing their health, my family, friends, and medical staff were both celebrating my awakening and mourning.

A few weeks after my "wake-up day," I received a package from my teacher that contained autographed copies of books authored by her and Fay Weldon. I had no idea she even remembered who I was or knew what was happening with me. I only took one class with her, and I was studying to be a teacher, not an English major, not a writer—and yet, she remembered me.

With one hand covering my slightly useless eye, I read what I could and played the *Phantom of the Opera* soundtrack over and over to soothe my soul. But more than anything, I used my sense of humor. When the ventilator was removed, I first asked "What the f— happened?" and my mother's response was "Yup, she's feeling better." I made inappropriate jokes about taking my temperature rectally before first buying me dinner until my doctor blushed and my nurses high-fived me. I cracked jokes in front of the interns and forced them, despite the head doctor's behavior, to introduce themselves, speak directly to me, and laugh. After another round of chemo and a stem cell transplant, I gained back the use of my legs and, to the embarrassment of my mother, pretended to walk into doors and told everyone the port catheter and trach scars were wounds from a gang-related fight. I even dyed my bald head with Easter egg dye—prompting my mom to lovingly call me an asshole when I said, "Look, Ma—I'm an egg!"

So even though I'm closer now than ever to a midlife crisis, I know this much: Keep watch for irrevocable moments, take up as much space as possible, and always find the humor in any situation.

How Radiation Helped Me Use My Voice

PAT MCGRATH

I had pictured the end of my treatments to be less taxing and go smoother than the trauma of surgery and the challenge of chemo. But that was not to be. Thankfully, I thought, radiation sessions will not take four and a half hours like surgery or drag on for five hours like each chemo infusion. Instead, radiation would take only eight minutes. Eight minutes sounded like a cakewalk, but I found out fast that each of those minutes could feel like an eternity.

For the past five months, all my caregivers had been women. Both surgery and chemo departments felt quiet, supportive, almost comforting. The radiation department, however, had more men, and their energy was very different. Maybe because they don't have a uterus, or maybe physics demands all their attention. Whatever the reason, to me the environment felt distant and remote. The communication was abrupt. For example, no one noticed my inner panic as they described how a cylinder would be placed inside of me (by the doctor) just before everyone else went into a separate room.

I was immediately reminded of giving birth (fifty years ago) at a time when all the OB-GYN doctors were men. Whenever they'd describe how I would (or should) feel, I could hear a voice inside my head go, "Objection, hearsay! These guys are never gonna know how this feels." Imagine my anxiety ramping up when a young male technician, sporting way too much testosterone, introduced himself in a booming voice. It was jarring.

He made small talk as I straddled a contraption on the table, designed to keep me motionless during the "simulation." The more he talked, the more trapped I felt. The doctor was a consummate professional while the female technician tried to help. However, neither said anything to this guy. In the old days, it was the kind of moment where females might question their own feelings. After all, "boys will be boys."

But the following week, as I walked into the treatment room dressed in a hospital gown and very anxious, the same technician yelled in from the hallway, "Hey, Patricia, remember me?" Truly, a "WTF" moment. That was it.

I had had enough.

I needed to focus, and this guy was demanding my attention.

This happened as I was simultaneously being introduced to two new people, a female technician and a male physicist. (Both were kind, empathetic, and aware.)

After thinking about it over the weekend, and talking to my friends, I called the nurse navigator. I told her I felt extremely uncomfortable, and since I had two more treatments to go through, I wanted a change. In short, I wanted him gone. Under the circumstances, his immaturity was too much for me. Maybe I was healing my younger self, intimidated by the all-male arena. Back then there was no recourse. Today, however, there are more options—and I'm older and wiser.

Melinda Gates, in her fabulous book *The Moment of Lift*, teaches us that when women are empowered to use their voice, the world changes and everyone benefits. (Feeling empowered is only possible when one feels worthy.) When I was first diagnosed, I set out to help my body help itself, but what I found out was that all the inner work I had previously been doing was now being called to task.

Until I faced this situation, I didn't even know I wasn't using my own voice to speak up. I was programmed to not "rock the boat." I now had an opportunity to use a different perspective, and for that I am grateful.

As I left the department after my last treatment, I told my favorite nurse about the call I had made. She looked at me as if she'd never had a patient take charge before and said, "I'm so glad you're being proactive. I really enjoyed working with you." Then despite our masks, and the COVID protocols, she gave me a hug.

We never know who else we may be helping by speaking up for ourselves. It was the least I could do for me and for any other woman who might follow. For now, I want to thank all of you for your love and support. It's time to focus on my well-being and celebrate the fact that I'm officially cancer free—yippee!

The Year of Living Cautiously After a Life of Living Large

NANCY BOCSKOR

During World War II, the federal government paid for the nursing education of young women to meet the overwhelming demand of care for the wounded in war hospitals overseas. In this accelerated program, students completed their RN degrees in two and a half years rather than the standard three. My mother, Phyllis Moberly Bocskor, graduated from Miami Valley Hospital and finished the program just as the war was ending, so she was not sent overseas despite being entirely ready to go.

Mom's been ready to go all her life, but what does being ready to go mean for a woman who is now ninety-five?

Mom originally wanted to attend Ohio State University's journalism school, but let's be clear; most women who even managed to scrape together the money during the Depression were offered three options: You became a nurse, a teacher, or a secretary.

Yet even though she never became a journalist, Mom always had a story.

She'll tell you, as if it happened yesterday, how she was a starter on the basketball team in Buford, Ohio, despite being barely five feet tall. Her 1939 team photo shows the female faces of determination, fierceness, and power. The joy was short-lived, however, because the Ohio State Board of Education soon after ruled that women were "too delicate" to play competitive sports.

She'll tell you about how her sixteenth birthday was December 8, 1941, the day after the attack on Pearl Harbor, and how most of her male friends immediately dropped out of high school to join the military. Many didn't return.

Mom's stories about her time as a nurse in the emergency room—"I had to act fast to help save lives"—still give her satisfaction.

Her time as a nurse also embedded something into her that didn't really have a name back then: feminism.

Mom tells the horror stories of women who either tried to end an unwanted pregnancy themselves or went to back-alley abortionists and ended up in the ER, hemorrhaging, infected, or dying. She also recalls the callousness of the male doctors towards rape victims: "She couldn't keep her legs closed." She was infuriated over the lack of control women had over their lives and their bodies. My mother has written checks to Planned Parenthood for more than half a century, and she'll tell you why.

Depression, poverty, and a grandmother who died after having eleven children before she was forty left deep scars—and it also instilled ambition.

When the war ended, the weddings began. Like all her friends, Mom married quickly. The marriage lasted seven years. This is a story she won't tell. She deflects by saying "he was a nice man" but she wanted earn her own money rather than have a family right away.

(Sidebar: I didn't know Mom was divorced until I was in eighth grade. She was at least ten years older than other mothers. I pitched a teenage fit about her being "old and mean" when she refused to let me wear a mini-skirt. She calmly responded that she had been married before. Yes, getting a divorce in the mid-'50s was so scandalous that my Hungarian Catholic father didn't want me to know.)

After I was born in 1957, Mom no longer worked full-time. She volunteered as a nurse, though, and organized trips for student groups and organizations until finally, to celebrate her fiftieth birthday, she took a trip to Europe for the first time. She went by herself and stayed for six weeks as part of a study-tour.

Flash forward to March 2020: Mom, who has used a walker since she broke her hip fifteen years ago, falls twice in February, and the woman who can still tell stories about her youth suffers from dementia. My sister and I are going to reluctantly move her to assisted living.

Then COVID numbers skyrocket.

Mom, my head cheerleader and self-appointed creator of "I'm not bossy, I have leadership skills," needed me more than the Texas university where I had launched a Center for Women in Politics & Public Policy in 2020.

I move back to my hometown to help care for her.

Fierce in our devotion to life and curiosity, I am the daughter-apple who has not fallen far from the mother-tree.

Firmly rooted and still growing, my mother and I face the next adventure.

Do Not Deal with a Woman Caparrotti

LAURA CAPARROTTI

"Do not deal with a woman Caparrotti," my grandfather Caparrotti used to say. I think he was referring to all the women in his life, though, not just the ones bearing his last name.

The first woman must have been my great-grandmother, a Rodino, who married into the family. According to my father, to manage the house and the family, she invented and performed a show for the entire town so no one could gossip about her not being able to manage the house. Almost every day, she appeared at the balcony of their house, lamenting that her husband, my great-grandfather, was not giving her enough money to buy food for the family. Following, my great-grandfather appeared on the other balcony, lamenting that his wife was stealing money from him. The truth was that my great-grandfather was leaving money in a drawer for her to find without having to ask so that he could still be considered the head of the house.

My own grandfather, their first son, grew up in this house with two brothers and three sisters. He became an anti-fascist, was in exile for twenty years, and then, as his mother wished, entered into an arranged marriage. The offspring of this union, my father and his sisters, all had big personalities. You knew when they were entering a room; they were remembered and sometimes feared, especially the women.

My aunt Eleonora, the oldest one, was fierce in the grandest way. She either adored you or deplored you. You could tell when she was ready to fight, as she turned slowly into an Italian Erinni. If she disliked you—and therefore disliked anything you said or did—she would stand on her feet and, with a clear, strong voice explain why you were absolutely wrong. A strong woman who fought with the Radical Party in Italy against inequality and for human rights, and who—to my surprise—followed some traditions far from her beliefs.

The fiercest of all women was not a Caparrotti, however; it was my mother, Luisa. She was the sweetest and the brightest person I have ever met.

She loved you with all the love possible if you were clear, honest, transparent, and not shady to her. She never raised her voice or her manners (well, she did sometimes, very elegantly, when I did something so annoying that even she was out of patience).

She was equally fierce in her sweetness and understanding. "I see everything, I say nothing," and that seeing everything was her strength. You knew she saw you and loved you anyway. The very few times she argued with my dad in front of me, she did it in silence. My father was playing the conscious victim, the one who knows he's making mistakes but, being a victim of his own weakness, is just sad and innocent because there is nothing to do about it. I saw her speaking to him with a steady voice, saying all the right words there were to say, leaving him (and me when it was my turn) completely destroyed inside because we had disappointed such a marvelous creature.

My mother was admired by everyone. She was beloved. Regarded as a strong, classy lady, she spoke only the necessary words. She was never closed-minded or traditional, she listened to everyone and gave her opinion on what she believed and never on what she was supposed to think.

When a friend of mine came out to her family and announced her marriage to the woman she loved, her own family refused to attend the wedding. But my mom offered to be her bridesmaid, adding that no one had the right to tell her whom to love or who to be.

She was fierce even in the last days of her life, my mother. She knew what was coming, yet she was busy comforting the rest of us—family and friends—because she could tell we were devastated by the thought of losing her.

"You have a great life to live, and you have so many things to do!" she was telling me with a smile while I was crying like crazy trying to ease my pain. "I lived my life, and I don't fear death." Was she was fierce in an Italian way or woman's way? She was fierce in her own way, a way never to be forgotten by anyone who ever met her.

The fiercest. The sweetest. My mom, Luisa.

What a Life!

JOAN SELIGER SIDNEY

I was born six weeks early in 1942. A nurse mis-weighed me at three and a half pounds, telling my mother I would die. For six weeks, she schlepped to the hospital to nurse her four-and-a-half-pound premie. I owed her from the start.

Only fifteen months before, my parents had escaped Hitler by fleeing halfway around the world. Though they kept quiet about their losses, loneliness pervaded our three rooms. I grew up feeling I needed to be perfect, to make up for grandparents and relatives I'd never know. An overachiever, I graduated from Abraham Lincoln High School with both French and Hebrew medals, as well as a diploma from Marshalliah Hebrew High School. Add features editor of the *Lincoln Log*, First Class Girl Scout, and pianist to my list. Although I wanted to attend a Seven Sisters college, Mom convinced me to live at home and take two trolleys to Brooklyn College.

"You're lucky," she said. "For high school, I had to live alone in another city. I starved. My overweight friend gave me half her sandwich for lunch and loaned me her books to study."

How could I disappoint Mom? To avoid temptation, I never applied elsewhere. But I hated Brooklyn College with my classmates from kindergarten. Salvation came when we moved to the Bronx and I transferred to CCNY. In their English Honors Program, I wrote my thesis on Virginia Woolf, and became a feminist.

For graduate school, Mom didn't ask me to turn down Harvard for a Master of Arts in Teaching on a full fellowship. But after a liberating year in Cambridge, my only job offer came from New Rochelle High School. I landed back in my Bronx bedroom. When, after my first year of teaching, I married my Harvard beau and moved to New Rochelle, Mom was dismayed.

"Aren't you and Stu going to live in your bedroom? If not for Hitler, I never would have left my parents."

"But this is America, Mom," was all I said. Besides having sex and barely sleeping, I taught five senior English classes in a row. Two nights a week I commuted to Manhattan to teach Freshman English at CCNY. Is it surprising that I felt exhausted? Six weeks later, numbness and tingling crept up my right foot and leg until I couldn't walk. Three and a half weeks of horrific hospital tests—in those days before MRIs—yielded nothing. "It might be birth control pills or a virus," the neurologist said. No contraceptive worked. In the next seven years, I gave birth to four children, and although I had signed up to be Connecticut's first legal abortion, I changed my mind. Choice is part of feminism. This led to my peak experience, giving birth in France by the Lamaze method during Stu's sabbatical.

Afterward, while raising my brood, I became a full-time doctoral student at the University of Connecticut. Instead of a teaching assistantship, I taught Lamaze Prepared Childbirth three nights a week. I kept extra busy punching cards at the computer center to evaluate my pre–post thesis project: "Reeducating a Generation of Teachers about Non-Sexist Attitudes and Curriculum."

Any surprise that I woke one night to numbness and tingling? I saw the neurologist my neighbor with multiple sclerosis (MS) recommended, and self-diagnosed. For the next nineteen years, I moved from denial to acceptance as the disease slowly progressed. My greatest challenge was telling my mother why I had trouble walking.

"Come live with me in Florida. I'll take care of you," she said.

"No, I love you, Mom, but my life's in Storrs."

Late '80s I did an MFA in poetry at Vermont College. Afterward I returned to France, teaching creative writing at l'Université de Grenoble. For eighteen months—with the help of incredible neighbors—I lived on my own in a mountainside apartment in the village of Venon, until MS progression put me in a wheelchair. This year, on May 7, I finished my first draft translating Mireille Gansel's *Maison D'Âme*. She's an award-winning poet and translator, also a second-generation Holocaust survivor. A mutual friend from Venon introduced us.

Besides many writing projects and part-time teaching, I've become an athlete. Because I'm in a high-tech wheelchair, to keep my body flexible, six mornings a week I swim half a mile at our local community center then hobnob in the locker room. I go therapeutic horseback riding every week to strengthen my core. Winter Saturdays you'll find me "shredding the gnar" in adaptive skiing. Black Diamonds here I come!

In Their Words

BETH BLATT

Sometimes, we just know. *This*, I am supposed to do. You feel it—a quickening in your heart, a deep knowing. You're not sure where you're going, but once you've had a glimpse of the journey ahead, how can you turn back?

> *You can have everything one day and then everything destroyed.*
> *So you have to be careful in life.*
> *I'm trying not to remember I'm a refugee;*
> *it makes me scared.*
> — *"R" (refugee woman from Haiti)*

This. I feel it when I join a group of theatre-making women in New York and hear about their new project: interviewing women refugees from around the world and crafting these into a theatrical presentation. They see it as a collage. I know it wants to be a play. I don't say this. But I do offer to set up and manage the Dropbox where all the materials will go.

We send a questionnaire to our international contacts who will connect us with refugee women. By the following April, we have received all of eight interviews, most only a few paragraphs long. We have sourced some other material—a poem, a monologue, an essay. Slim pickings. I am busy elsewhere, and my quickening has slowed.

My co-creators say we can't get this together in less than eight weeks, in time for World Refugee Day.

Of course we can. *This* I can do. I don't say it yet, but I think it.

THE UNIVERSE PROVIDES

Here I go all woo-woo (so sue me). Magical connections appear. The president of a global women's organization (turns out we share an alma mater) sends me interviews with three refugee women in Syria. A colleague locates a Burmese woman in Albany. On these bones, there is good meat.

May 1. Six weeks until World Refugee Day. I've fallen under the spell of Moo Paw from Burma, Shireen from Syria. I go a bit rogue.

IN PRAISE OF DEADLINES

May 18. I book a venue. Sign a contract. No going back. I have four weeks to make a play. To get actors to act it. To entice people to see it. To let these women be heard.

BEGINNER'S MIND

Have I mentioned I've never written a play? Musicals, yes. A few ten-minute playlets, the odd monologue. But not a real play.

I don't have the skills—or time—to get fancy. I remember a mentor's words: Let the content dictate the form. I look for connections in the stories: shared words, sentiments, events. I opt for simple; organize it by chapters: Before. But Then. Trapped. And Then. Now.

June 1, Draft 1.

These past-tense narratives must come to life. I switch verbs to the present. Have actors step into one another's stories, reenact them. Frame it with hope: Some of these women make it to safety. To America.

June 3, Draft 2.

The process is more listening than writing. I'm a seamstress, stitching their perfect words together, verbatim.

Since I've never done this before, the bar is mercifully low. Done is better than good.

THE UNIVERSE PROVIDES—AGAIN

June 3. I chance to meet a caterer who employs refugee women. Score!

June 8. Interview R, a fragile but resolute refugee from Haiti.

June 9. T from Honduras.

Then C arrives: HIV-positive, Rwandan genocide survivor. Fiery and fierce. Just what we need.

June 10, Draft 3. Rip apart the tapestry I've made; integrate the new material.

June 17, Draft 9. Today's our one rehearsal. The shortcomings are stunning. Still, I have time. Three days.

June 20, 10:52 a.m., Draft 11. "In Her Words Final."

7:00 p.m. Somehow, it is standing room only.

As we start, R slips in quietly. My stomach drops. What if I got her wrong?

But then, as it must, the show goes on. Afterward, the talkback goes on longer than the play. I take pages of notes. They want more of this, more of that. More work to do. I can't wait.

The next day I receive an email from R:

It was a pleasure to be there yesterday. To open up a little bit about my story, I feel that I'm relieved. I understand that I'm not the only one who've been through that sort of situation. Even if we're from separate place, our story is similar. Thanks Beth.

No, thank you. For *This*.

Close

LOUISA BALLHAUS

Driving down I-91 with a manic gleam in my eyes, I am in the midst of a rare episode in which I operate outside of shame and self-reflection. I have been sweating profusely for nearly an hour and talking incessantly about it ever since Harry got in the car. I have just made him touch the sweat, lay his hand somewhere close to my heart and feel the sheer volume of liquid, insisting that it would relieve the tension we'd *clearly both been feeling* to have him admit that, yes, I was in fact *very sweaty.*

Really, I just needed someone to wade into my increasingly absurd reality for a moment and experience it with me, to tell me we were living through the same thing.

It was nice to have someone close. It had been so long.

• • •

Harry's younger sister tried to kill herself when she was thirteen. He refers to it as *something stupid she did* and says all he remembers is riding in the front of the ambulance. When he tells me, I feel a surge of protective emotion, a desire to wrap my arms between his body and the pain the world is waiting to inflict—has already inflicted.

Days later, he asks with perfect calm if all my burns are accidental. He reacts as I like people to in this particular instance (invisibly) when I say: most.

• • •

The twenty-minute drive from Harry's campus to mine takes forty, but I can't stop smiling. He holds my sweating, shaking hand and acts like nothing is happening at all. The only time he flinches is when we pull into my driveway and I shriek with joy at the sight of a groundhog, an old friend.

Even that, I never would have known his reaction, but he tells me later that day: *I thought I was going to die in that moment, when I heard you scream.* I laugh at him. *In that moment? After that drive?* I had been hysterical. I had had no business being on the road. He agrees but he doesn't care. It was just the groundhog that got him.

• • •

After Harry asks about my burns, I show him the cuts too. He says he already knew I cut myself. That he was just curious if I burned myself too. It makes me hate him. I ask him how his sister tried to kill herself, but he doesn't want to talk about it.

The way he had asked about my burns was perfect. He is very close to how I want him to be.

• • •

Harry says his ex-girlfriend cheated on him after eight months, but I feel like they were together longer. He has a stuffed horse from her in his bottom drawer and a series of letters she wrote for his time away, labeled with directives like "open if you're feeling sad" or "open if you miss me." He tells me where to find them—*only because I know you'll find them anyway*—and I admire her penmanship when I read them.

That night, he comes back from his flying lesson and we do drugs until his nose bleeds and he blames it on the altitude.

We whisper "I'm so lucky" back to each other until I can pretend I didn't say it first.

• • •

Sometimes, when I am alone with Harry, I run my fingers through his hair and struggle not to think the word "prey." I want so much from him, I worry there will be nothing left when I am done. I had thought my heart would explode on the highway, shirt clinging heavy and damp to my ribs, as he wrapped his hand around my sweaty fingers and I counted out the choice every second he didn't let go.

Perfectly Imperfect

MONA FRIEDLAND

Is it true that all behaviors can be traced back to our mothers? Why is it that psychiatrists and psychologists spend half their billable hours explaining how our parents influenced our attitudes, behaviors, and personality traits? Can we possibly undo the distinguishing features they passed along to us, whether we wanted to be defined by them or not?

Growing up in a household where everything had its place, I acquired my mother's tendencies toward perfectionism. What's saved me is that I've acknowledged and accepted my role as an "imperfect perfectionist" and learned not to judge my habits too harshly. I'd never judge any of my friends as harshly as I judge myself, so I've learned to be kinder when looking at my own behaviors, especially since I've crafted some perspective about them.

As a young child, my mother recently related to me, I would come inside for a nap after playing in our sandbox. I was probably no more than three or four at the time, and yet, even in those toddler years, I would undress carefully, fold my sandy clothes neatly, and place them tidily on my chair. What four-year-old does this?

My mother swears she never told me to do this, but I am doubtful. I didn't learn this from watching *Gilligan's Island*.

Today I sometimes wonder if the things I do would be labeled "compulsive" or considered part of an "OCD" spectrum; the professional perfectionists in our culture seem to want to define people like me. Do I have to fit into a category? Did my mother put me there?

Making a list of things to do for the day? Make sure you check off what has been accomplished—or rewrite the list so it is neat and orderly? Yes.

The home in which I grew up was obsessed with neatness. Having company over for dinner? Make sure all the wastebaskets have been emptied, because the home should look like NOBODY lives here. I still do this every time I expect anyone to visit.

Changing your clothes during the day? Do not under any circumstances place your worn clothes on a chair or the bed. They must be immediately hung in the closet so that your room is ready for inspection by the Queen. Done.

How do I know this is a family thing? My brother, Marshal, suffers from the same malady. Making his bed at five years old, he would pull the bed away from the wall and then run around, tucking all the edges in so they were perfectly aligned. He also needed my mother, the House General, to approve of him. My mother said it was "so cute when he did that," but I'm sure that she was silently applauding his lifetime membership in the Perfectionist Club at 28 Steven Street. On a positive note, my brother is a great dinner guest, as he is willing to wash every single dish and also clean off the countertops better than a person you would pay to clean your house.

My husband likes to say that parents don't get up in the morning and say, "How can we screw up the kids today?" Almost all parents do the best they can, using their own parents as role models. Our parents' generation didn't read Dr. Spock or listen to any other experts while raising us; they didn't have the benefit of countless articles on child-rearing, parenting, or good psychological hygiene.

Is it a surprise that they kept tidy and free from the messiness they could see in their homes and didn't focus on the "hidden child"?

My mother and her generation did what they thought was, well, perfect.

And while our parents might not have done it perfectly, we grew up to be caring, functioning adults, raising our own children and trying to make the world a better place. While some of these values were our own, we children of the '60s, we have clearly been influenced by our parents' values, strengths, and shortcomings.

Gratitude is on the top of the list I keep (and rewrite neatly) for every new day; recognizing our glorious imperfection comes right after.

The Inheritance

SUZY JOHNSON

My mom died last December. She'd been in an assisted living home near Knoxville, Tennessee, where my sister and brother and I grew up in a subdivision called Village Green. My parents moved to Knoxville from Memphis (where I was born) in 1971.

I'd seldom seen or spoken to my mom after she suffered a brain aneurysm in 2005. We were leaning toward estrangement even before then, and while the rock-star brain surgeon at Vanderbilt Hospital was able to save her life, he wasn't able to do any rewiring that would repair our relationship. A few years later, I was informed that my mom had legally disinherited me.

She was eighty-six when she died, so we weren't surprised. But that's not to say I knew how or what to feel about her death. When we learned the end was near, I called her; her tone remained brusque. Imperious. She was at least consistent. There would be no end-of-life reconciliation, and in some ways I respect that more. It's truthful.

Still, I committed to embracing better memories of my mom and ventured to Google articles in her community paper to find evidence of happier times. I started searching for old news stories about her Red Hat Society; surely there was a photo of her chapter at, say, the Cracker Barrel, decked out in their purple outfits and red hats, eating steak and biscuits.

After trying various queries and word combos—I mean, who's to say what algorithm will yield the complexity of a mother?—an article from 2013 surprised my search, including a photo of my mom in her signature purple velour pantsuit, sitting at her assisted living home's piano, beaming for the camera.

I'd never seen it. Never been told about it. My cursor stopped, then moved ahead with the force of unearthing the priceless artifact of an ancient queen.

In her interview with a local reporter, my mom describes—are you sitting down, reader?—her long friendship with ... ELVIS! Yes, that Elvis. As in, The King.

It was the OMG of OMGs. I couldn't believe what I was reading. Or could I?

When we were growing up, my mom, taking a slow drag off her Tareyton cigarette, would occasionally reminisce about playing piano at a venue in Memphis and seeing Elvis's manager, Colonel Tom Parker, once. But there was no claim she knew Elvis. I remember watching the repeat of *Hogan's Heroes* after school in 1977 and yelling into the kitchen, "Elvis died!" when the news scroll ran across the TV, which may have elicited a mild shock but no memorable outpouring of emotion or grief. Yet somehow, a brush with the Colonel had morphed into friends-with-Elvis (presumably without benefits)—and it got published! I'm also told she was known to humble-brag in her assisted living home that Elvis, you know, confided in her when he and Priscilla divorced.

What a testament to the charming, commanding presence of my mom. It was completely on-brand for her.

For me, discovering this hidden gem of my mom's psyche required some processing. In the end I decided it didn't matter if my mom knew Elvis or truly believed she was friends-with-Elvis. She suffered from unexplored emotional issues most of her life, and crafting narratives to gain the affection she felt she lacked was one of her many coping mechanisms. She's not the first to look back on a life of limited choices and feel some regret as she raised daughters who, in her mind, could seemingly have it all.

Determined to focus on the surplus of amusement that could be found in all this, I wondered what my own celebrity artist friendship might be in later years. Friends-with-Sting? Madonna? Prince? My mind went round and round with possibilities until finally I realized, *No, I'm good.* I don't want or need the validation of a celebrity friendship to know my story is abundant with choices that add up to anything but ordinary. Nobody has it all, but my failures, successes, relationships, and everything in between, I've crafted it all. I've exercised my agency IRL, as the kids say, and I'm pretty pleased with those results.

My mother died without understanding how her perception of her own life gifted an ample inheritance to me. But maybe she and Elvis are chatting about it on the lush, plentiful grounds of Graceland.

Rage Begins at Home

MARY ANN CAWS

Dedicated to the memory of Carolyn Heilbrun

What to do with anger?

Sylvia Plath, *Journal* (May 20, 1958)

Energy comes from and is sometimes indistinguishable from a rage I mean to speak of. I will not be distinguishing between rage and anger, for I believe they have me both, and use me as much as I use them. To start with, I begin enraged at myself, for it still does not come easily, after all these years, the speaking *out* or *up* that others seem to do. I often do not know how to take up my own place in the world, even in the academy, unless I am asked. You would think I thought I had to be invited after all these years, to be invited to be at home. After doing a lot of time, if you see what I mean. I have, I do swear it, done my time. Is this being a Southern female? I typify the genre. The genre itself may be just that *home* I want eventually to write.

• • •

So I will write here a little history of my rage. I had an angry father. Upright and upstanding, he had a sense of humor, but an anger such as I have seen rarely since. It was oddly allied to his affection for my sister and myself. Something about growing up with rage around you leads to your seeking it out later. Any therapist could have told me that, but seeking help just wasn't done where I came from. Actually, most things, or so it seemed for ages, just weren't done where I live in my mind, even when I no longer live there.

And then I became attached, years later, to an angry genius of a Provençal poet whose translator and interpreter I became. Attached with my whole mind and the heart it finally proves itself to be if you trust it long enough. Attached to a storming force of nature in a countryside of light arage. So I spent quite a bit of my adult life, just like my life as a child, in tears. Unable to speak, I could only write. This poet I translated and wrote so much on, this poet I loved for his poetry and his face, and his mountainousness, was in himself as vast as he was unforgiving, massive in anger as in love.

Finally, at least in this brief story, I married an English philosopher with an anger contained inside, as if repeating my history with my father and my poet. About people, I never learned to ask anything. Of them, perhaps a bit more. Just like Parsifal, I had not learned to ask questions, and it stood me in very bad stead indeed. It is, now that I reflect upon it, as if the triple rage of the men closest to me had taken my tongue forever. So much for the beginnings of the rage in practice around me, and my nonresponse. Answer calls, I think, for practice. Rage must learn to respond to rage, in which practice I am still, as I said, at my beginnings. Like a would-be knight unarmed, ready to set out if I could just figure out where you were supposed to go quest.

I have not learned anger completely enough, and do not even know if I am still weeping inside. I think perhaps so. My poet is dead, my father is dead, my marriage was split open—"these bonds," we once said to each other, "are of bronze and cannot be broken"—but they are. Is it now my anger I must muster, now that I weep no longer outside, or is it something else?

• • •

Here is what I suspect it is: a deeply personal energy nourished by the anger that has not always learned to speak its name. Yet some things Southern females finally speak, slowly, with sudden determination.

I have lost all those three males, each in a separate time, and each was full of anger—and I have gained something I am learning to call myself. This energy must lead to expression. I know now *why* beauty has to—as Breton has it—be convulsive, or not be. I know it from inside. As for my personal rage, it no doubt contributes also to what I write, read, speak. It is at the origin, albeit implicitly, of the sort of personal criticism I undertake and share in with others.

Middle Sister

PIA L. BERTUCCI

Human geographers emphasize the significance of urban centers for a people's emotional and social history. "Phantasmagoria," coined by Steve Pile, references emotions, imagination, ghosts, and physical space that shape city dwellers' identities. Although my two sisters and I have only been in communication for the past decade, I now view our lifetime memories as mingling in a liminal space that always existed.

In the fall of 1987, I would walk from my receptionist job at a downtown Chicago law firm to Union Station, passing the Bennigan's on Michigan Avenue. The icy darkness I was rushing through contrasted with the celebratory light encircling the diners and drinkers inside, representing a world I felt removed from. Single, pregnant, and alone, I had exiled myself from most of my friends and family. My life consisted of work, college classes, and an all-consuming anxiety over my future. Little did I know that one of the servers in that restaurant represented a parallel life dilemma from another dimension.

At that time, and up until eleven years ago, I was the oldest of two sisters. As far as I knew.

On Friday, August 27, 2010, I received a letter bearing only the sender's first name; I almost discarded it as junk mail.

I now believe some metaphysical force was directing me to open it, to take one critical step that would forever alter my perception of my life.

• • •

The letter was written by a "confidential intermediary" and referenced a "Midwest Adoption Center":

"You may be an important person in the life of someone who is seeking to locate their birth relatives."

The intermediary cited a circuit court judge and Illinois adoption laws removing any lingering doubt of the letter's legitimacy. The missive went on to vaguely explain that the subject in question was an adult woman. There was no indication of her relationship to my family.

I immediately called my sister, Anna. She did not waste time with *hello*: "Did you get the letter?" she asked.

Since it was too late to call the Chicago office until Monday, we discussed myriad possibilities as to who the subject of the letter could be: a random cousin perhaps?

The following Monday, in a phone call, the intermediary confirmed what I had suspected. I granted the intermediary permission to share my contact details with my "new" sister, Sonja.

In the protracted hours before Sonja's call, Anna and I spoke again. Being the more rational one, Anna posed the question, *What is a sister? Someone simply linked to you by DNA? Or someone with whom you shared top-bunk "Window Shade Movies," Saturday morning Barbie encampments in the living room, running from the infamous neighborhood bullies the "tomato boys" (so-called because they raided people's gardens and wielded vegetables like weapons), falling into a frozen Lake Michigan with cousins and living to tell (albeit disparate versions of) the tale?* Then there was the time that I, aged six, single-handedly "sprung" my three-year old sister from preschool and brought her to day camp with me for the rest of the summer. (Nobody questioned us; it was the 1970s.) Anna and I shared a lifetime of memories as sisters that Sonja was not a part of. And yet, when I finally did talk to Sonja, I realized how many times our paths could have crossed: field trips to the Museum of Science and Industry, afternoons at 12th Street Beach, and countless other urban nexuses on the South Side, where she also grew up, just a few miles away. And then there was Bennigan's, where Sonja was a server in the fall of 1987.

My mind has refashioned so many memories: Young Sonja and I bump into each other in the "Yesterday's Main Street" exhibit at the museum; Anna and I borrow Sonja's shovel at the beach; I stare right at Sonja through that window in Bennigan's and she nods at me with a tacit understanding.

On Thanksgiving of 2015, our families met up at my parents' lake house for a feast of combined culinary forces representing our collective as well as individual backgrounds: shrimp and grits, various pastas, and Baba's (our great-grandmother) stuffing. Photographic evidence of the event includes a video of we three sisters on the beach that night, emboldened by Prosecco, performing iPhone karaoke of our collective history of '80s music. We sang "Kiss on My List" as though we had sung it a hundred times together. I think I remember they were playing it one night at Bennigan's.

Writing Saved Me

JANE COOK

It was 1972 and I was just out of college with a BA in English and a secondary English teaching certificate. I was eager to start my career, but there were no middle or high school jobs to be had. Still, the landlord wouldn't wait for the rent, and I needed to eat and pay the electricity and phone bills. So, I set off to find any job I could.

After some unsuccessful attempts, one day a neighbor who worked at a local university told me he needed to hire a van driver. David worked in a department that trained administrators from developing countries. These administrators needed to be transported from their apartments to their various trainings all week. On weekends, they were taken on sightseeing trips around New England to get what the university considered to be "a flavor of the United States."

I liked to drive. I needed a job. David was desperate. He hired me on the spot. The next day, I went to the Motor Vehicle Department, took a driving test, passed it, and was issued a Public Service License. That permitted me to drive a passenger van for my new job; I was officially a Student Driver.

I enjoyed interacting with the administrators who were visiting the campus, and although it wasn't teaching, I liked it. I gave many of them English lessons during our lunch hours. We often played tennis together after work.

Despite not doing the work for which I was trained, I was enjoying myself until Vic (I've changed his name to rhyme with a word that matched his personality), the program's director, learned that I could type. He decided he could make use of me inside his office. Dubbing me "Super Student Driver," which was certainly unofficial, Vic pulled me away from the steering and tossed me into the secretarial pool. I took the state typing exam, which I aced at one hundred words per minute with 99 percent accuracy. He offered me a full-time job as a Typist II. Because it came with a slight pay increase and good medical benefits, I took it.

At first Vic seemed harmless enough, but it didn't take me long to learn that he was a misogynist and a bully. He delighted in yelling at the women in the secretarial pool and on an almost daily basis, reduced at least one of them to tears.

But he didn't do that to me.

When the professors ran a two-week simulation for the administrator trainees, I participated by organizing my female colleagues. We drew a cartoon showing a Male Chauvinist Pig (MCP) cracking a whip and wrote articles and a poem for the *Daily Independent*, the newspaper I typed during the simulation.

I took a day off during the simulation, which tactically was a good move, because one of the men had to type the newspaper that day.

I picketed in front of the building even though I was unsuccessful in getting my female colleagues to walk out too. The professors and trainees thought it was very funny, but I was a passionate feminist.

I was not joking.

One day Vic assigned me to type a high-stakes grant proposal that was due the next day. As I typed, I found his almost illegible handwriting riddled with errors—misspellings, poor word choices, grammar and usage errors. My fingers could not type them. I respectfully corrected the errors and handed back his original with my typed copy, proud to have done a good job.

Two hours later, he called me into his office and slammed the door. With clenched fists, he pounded his desk and ranted at me. As he dismissed me from his office, he screamed, "How dare you change my words. I pay you to type, NOT to edit my work. Don't ever do this again!" I walked out with my head bowed low, but I did not cry.

Since Vic hadn't fired me outright, I showed up for work the next day, anticipating a formal firing. When he called me into his office, I steeled myself for it. He said in an almost jovial voice, "You're not going to believe this, but my colleagues read my proposal and they said it's the best piece of writing I've ever done. From now on, I want you to edit everything I write."

Oh, I did believe it.

And I did continue to edit his writing—all of it. After that, when he started ranting in the office, I would look him straight in the eye and say, "F U, Vic." He would shake his head and walk away laughing.

I remained until I figured out how to save myself by transferring to another department. I don't know who edited his work after that, but I knew I had to write him out of my own story.

I May Be a Karen

GEORGIA COURT

I may be a Karen, but at least I'm cool.

I used to worry about not "getting" it. Recently I was worried about whether I might be a "Karen" after my son explained what it meant. I was horrified to realize that I actually am a Karen. Yikes!

I thought Karen was simply the name of a rather nice woman I know, a poetry teacher who lives in a place in the north where I spend my summers. (I have at least learned not to use "summer" as a verb.) So the word conjures up pleasant images of cool breezes on shady porches. But, no, it turns out that a Karen is what I am.

My son explained that a Karen is a boomer (guilty!). She's a white woman who believes the world cannot spin properly without her judgmental advice, and that advice usually comes in the form of a whining complaint. Oh, dear (guilty!). If I were to die now in some horrific accident, like if someone tired of hearing me complain pushed me off an eleventh-floor condo balcony, I know what I'd see flash before my eyes on my way down to splat on the sidewalk.

I'd see all those times I wailed about the installation of parking meters in our town—imagine putting them right on the street in front of my favorite store? And what about that favorite store? How many times has the proprietor heard me fuss about the clothing she carries? She can't ever seem to figure out which party attire I want. Don't you agree that cocktail dresses are cut too low at the top and too tight in the derriere? Well . . . surely that's something worthy of a hardy complaint. Now I know I was being a Karen. Am I going to be subjected to reliving that revelation on the way to the great beyond?

I won't even go into my memories about insisting waiters move me from table to table in my quest to find the best view out the window, the least-drafty seat away from an air vent, or the quietest spot far removed from the jazz quintet.

But, maybe more important than whether I am a Karen, I worried if I was "woke"? I thought I was. I thought I had plenty of empathy, thought I kept up with the times, thought I knew what side to be on regardless of which protest march was happening in town. But I now know the concept of woke includes the idea of "buy-in," and that it's not enough to show up to march with my friends and hold up a sign with a slogan. So, since I'm not really ready to completely buy in to everybody else's reality, I guess I'll skip that and focus on buying into my own reality.

My own reality, the way I see it, is that I am the coolest person I know, acknowledging that even using the word "cool" hopelessly dates me. Why am I so cool? Because I own a bookstore. It's a happy place for me since I love books, and I think it's a happy place for my customers as well. I opened a bookstore because there wasn't an indie in my town, and I simply wanted it for me. Nobody was stepping up to give me a bookstore; so I gave myself one. Now, much to my amazement and delight, books are like the coolest things out there. Ads feature gorgeous models with book in hand, any brand enhanced by the notion that people with both beauty and brains love whatever the advertiser is selling.

Well, that's something I can buy into. I am fully woke to the pleasure of books; and while I'm immersed in a good novel, who cares what the twenty-something down the street calls me.

Knicks Chick

LIA LEVITT

I honestly didn't know the Knicks were a basketball team, but I knew I loved the guy with the hat. OK, perhaps I didn't understand love in seventh grade or basketball. His piercing blue eyes matched the blue on the hat, and I decided it was the ticket to impressing him. I asked another boy in the hall, who chided me as if the Knicks being a basketball team was as obvious as my crush. The entire school, my grandparents, retired teachers, and everyone knew about my crush, except the guy I was determined to kiss.

My father rejected my plea to change the channel to the Knicks. "We don't watch basketball in this house."

I needed to learn. I started recording the games and studying as I would for any other school assignment. I learned about fouls, free throws, and free agents. I watched diligently until it was no longer a mission to impress; the Knicks had impressed me.

"Hey, did you see the Knicks game last night?"

"You like the Knicks?"

"Of course, who doesn't?"

I could've used my own sweat mop guy, the men who scurry on the court during time-outs to wipe up the players' sweat, when I finally broached the question to my crush. Thankfully, I passed as a basketball fan and, somehow, I unexpectedly now was one.

I began showing interest in playing with the guys from my neighborhood. I asked for a hoop above the garage for my birthday, and a coach began giving me some pointers. I had a promising layup and a promising friendship brewing with my crush. When my parents stopped the coaching, citing "I'd never get taller," I was deflated, but I still had my Knicks and hopes for Blue Eyes.

I approached my crush like I'd come to approach everything I'm passionate about—with fervent dedication, methodical research, and unwavering gusto. He smiled back, and that was all I needed to keep hoping.

Ewing, Starks, LJ, Mason, and Spreewell were my guys. Sure, they didn't win all the time—or sometimes all that often—but I didn't either. The Knicks were tall, talented, and provoked me to scream at my TV while romanticizing my first kiss with Blue Eyes.

"Yes, I will call" was scrawled in his handwriting on the note my friend gave me for my birthday a few years into my obsessive crush, now in high school. He didn't. There was hope, though, when he came to my sweet sixteen. I asked him to prom even though I had a serious boyfriend. He went alone, and I went in a Honda Civic. He signed my yearbook and wasn't my first or second kiss. I almost didn't graduate because I couldn't pass even makeup gym. Still, basketball was in my blood now, even just as a spectator.

An upsetting night led to a worse decision to take three shots at a local club in our hometown. I saw his friend coming out of the men's room and was elated to confirm he was here. At twenty-one, I was more confident and nine years into my crush. I promised myself if I could just get him alone, I'd make my move. I tried to entice him to come outside with me, and he seemed scared. I was relentless. Teenage life was torture, and I was on the precipice of greatness (or so I hoped), finally having my own place and direction.

I pushed open those doors with my little five-foot-nothing horsepower to my destiny and, finally alone, hooked my leg into his, grabbed his shirt collar, and kissed him. I didn't see stars. He was not a good kisser! My dreams weren't crushed, because I'd accomplished my nine-year goal. He was into it, and now I kinda wasn't. Maybe I didn't get the guy, but I got the men. I got the Knicks.

The Knicks made the playoffs in 2013, and I watched them win live. My patience was challenged again as I waited eight years until, on the cusp of pandemic restrictions lifting, they made fourth seed in the East. With my vaccination card in hand, and my four-inch orange-velvet, rhinestone-encrusted NYK wedges on foot, I was at game one. The shoes got me on the NYC news. I finally got to publicly declare I was the biggest female Knicks fan in the world. If only Blue Eyes knew he had sparked my most unexpected love, and it wasn't him; it was them.

A-L-C-O-H-O-L

FAITH PEASE

I learned how to spell faster than most kids. My family ate dinner together every night at 7:00 p.m., watching *Wheel of Fortune* on our tiny Sony TV. I saw how letters and words fit together.

By age five, my parents couldn't spell across me anymore. Gone were the days of spelling out P-LA-Y-G-R-O-U-N-D, in hopes I wouldn't understand.

I also learned that alcohol was not welcome in our house. There were no glasses of wine next to my mom at dinner. My parents didn't have other couples over for parties. Twenty-five years sober, and still counting, my parents had lost their drinking friends.

My parents' drunken adolescent tales were punctuated by Vanna White turning each vowel. By the time I was in middle school, I learned that my grandfather was abusive, using my dad and my aunts as his targets. I knew my mom had been homeless in San Francisco. I also recognized that alcoholism soaked deep into both sides of my family tree. The stories my parents told me were scary. Foreign words and phrases like *police, blackouts*, and *sleeping in a moving van on the side of the road*. They didn't fit together like the words on TV.

What made them fit together was A-L-C-O-H-O-L.

Sophomore year of high school, I began seeing a therapist because I couldn't handle my anxiety alone. She told me one thing that I needed to understand about myself: I was a child of alcoholics. She said, "Whether they are addicted to alcohol or any other substance, addicts almost never shake their addiction. It becomes redirected." When I got home later that day, I looked at the boxes of Poland Spring seltzers my dad drank every day and my mom's chocolate stash. I realized they had redirected. I remember feeling lucky that it was seltzer and sweets.

They made choices about how they were going to live in order to move forward.

The same year I started therapy, my friends started stealing vodka from their parents. They had a trick: Fill the bottle back up with water, and hope they won't notice. I did not have any vodka to steal, and my parents' drinking stories terrified me. I put orange juice in my water bottle and pretended it was spiked.

Alcohol made me a liar.

I took my first shot senior year of high school.

The summer before my freshman year of college, my dad bought me a pack of Mike's Hards. He said, "Don't let any boy tell you your limit." Little did he know I had already started drinking. I had learned my limit. I had also learned I didn't know when to stop.

When you're young, all you want to be is older. All you want to do is arrive at each milestone. Some people drink every day, and every night. Some can't stop when they start: One shot becomes six, and you wake up not remembering what you did, who you saw, or what you said.

It's scary. Maybe it is a college thing, and some will grow out of it, but my eight-year-old self remembers what my parents told me at the dinner table: Alcoholism runs in our family.

I want to be able to have a healthy relationship with alcohol, but I don't know if that's possible.

I am a child of two parents who had the strength, resilience, and power to overcome their addiction to drugs and alcohol. However, the absence of alcohol is loud.

They say in recovery that it takes one day at a time. Twenty-five years of taking it day by day, and my parents have built a life they are proud of. That I am proud of. I want to remember my life. The good, the bad, and everything that comes in between.

I know that each day, as I work on myself, I have almost A-R-R-I-V-E-D.

Plot Twist

SALLY KOSLOW

Had my great-grandmother had not lived in Minsk, she might have read *McCall's*, which began in 1873 and lasted for 124 years. Along with *Good Housekeeping, Ladies Home Journal, Redbook, Woman's Day, Family Circle,* and *Better Homes & Gardens*, it was one of the venerable Seven Sisters magazines. I was its last editor-in-chief.

To be honest, when I took over *McCall's*, its glory days were in the past, when girls played with Betsy McCall paper dolls, not video games. But it was still a swell job for the editor of the high school newspaper in Fargo. I'd grown up with the *McCall's* reader and, as a wife and mother, in many ways, was her (my meat loaf secret: applesauce). Magazines had taught me how to dress, spot skin cancer, and handicap the marriage prospects of Prince Charles.

At *McCall's* I loved publishing disease-of-the-month articles that saved people's lives; sharpening flaccid manuscripts; hiring smart people—women, mostly; popping in at celebrity cover shoots. The perks were appealing: discounts at posh hairdressers, tropical retreats, first-class travel to Paris, White House visits, and TV appearances.

When the time came for *McCall's* to get a facelift, I worked with a big-shot designer, followed by a presentation to about twenty of the company's business wonks. I unveiled each board, then waited for a response in a room so quiet I heard someone suck an Altoid.

"Great job," said the company's new president. (Let's call him Ira, because I hate that name.)

"You all know Rosie O'Donnell." Ira flashed a wolfish grin. "When she endorses a product, it flies off the shelf. If she had her own magazine, her celebrity friends would be on the cover."

Ira eventually invoked the name of Oprah, whose eponymous magazine was one of the biggest triumphs the industry had seen. Both he and Rosie clearly had Oprah-envy, writ large. Ira asked for opinions. Each sycophant around the conference table praised the idea—until they got to me.

"You can't compare Rosie to Oprah," I observed. "Any woman can artic-ulate what Oprah stands for—how to enhance your self-esteem, live your best life, show gratitude. It's a relatable message and natural magazine material. Rosie? She's sharp and funny (*and acerbic!*) but not the same golden goose."

Some genius then blurted out, "What if we gave Rosie *McCall's* and changed its name to *Rosie?*"

Quicker than you can say throw-the-bitch-under-the-bus, Ira struck a deal—with Rosie as an investor—to do just that. I was kicked upstairs to a nook with glass walls where I felt as exposed as a monkey at the zoo. I need not have worried about colleagues passing by to gawk, however. They avoided me altogether.

No sane person goes into the magazine industry expecting lifetime employment, but my situation was bizarre. Ira gave me the title of "editorial director," which turned out to be the Potemkin Village of jobs, with virtually no responsibility.

I refused to quit. It wasn't my fault that Ira was the crazy uncle who gave Rosie a magazine. There was also money on the table, and I had a child in college and bills to pay. If I resigned I'd get no severance, and probably no unemployment insurance. I filled my endless days with fake-work.

Did I mention I hated this job? No problem because, soon, it ended. I slunk back to job hunting.

Friends urged me to throw myself into one of my "hobbies." I'd raised two sons while I worked 24/7. Full stop. I had no hobbies. But in order to see people other than my husband, I enrolled in a writing workshop. My initial submission was a piece of fiction about a Chanel sample sale.

I, who'd liked nothing better than writing seven-word cover lines, sur-prised myself by finding the bandwidth to write a 355-page book about a midwestern magazine editor who gets shunted aside by a hotheaded celeb-rity. It sold to Putnam in a preemptive bid from an editor whose claim to fame was discovering *Peyton Place* in the slush pile.

I decided that perhaps the universe was sending me a message, and— plot twist!—I switched gears. Subsequently, I've published four more con-temporary novels, a historical novel, a nonfiction book, and many essays. Another novel and some kids' books are in utero.

Now, when I want to catch my breath, I stop in the middle of a paragraph, walk to the park—and think, *This is sweet, this book-writing thing.*

Why didn't I start it sooner?

The So-What Factor

FIONA PITT-KETHLEY

I got sent to Child Guidance at the age of seven. First, it was to a Harley Street psychologist on the orders of my headmistress, who was far more in need of help of that kind than I was. The psychologist suggested Child Guidance would cost nothing, which was better and very decent of her. The reason I was sent in the first place was because I wrote "bum" on someone's desk in pencil. It could be easily washed off. It wasn't even carved. But I wasn't supposed to know such a word at seven.

I enjoyed my weekly time playing at Child Guidance, as it meant one less afternoon at school. The psychologists were easy to lead by the nose. I set up a scenario in their doll's house and pretended I was worried my parents might take lodgers. They swallowed it hook, line, and sinker. I did this in case there was anything genuinely wrong with me. If there was, I wanted to keep it and not have them tampering with my personality.

I almost blew my cover when I played too long in the sandpit and set up a city's drainage system. I remembered my tale and got out in time. It was all part of the so-what factor, brazening things out. It is something women especially need to learn as we are chipped away at in education and the media. Sometimes it is men doing it to us, or sometimes it is the sisterhood. We are meant to be deferential and unsure of ourselves, and that is our undoing.

I didn't term it the so-what factor until an incident later in my life. When I was in my early twenties, I was still living with my mother. A builder had got planning permission to build alongside our house. We and others had objected at a council meeting, but it went ahead anyway. He was building two small houses in a plot that cut off the gardens of neighbors. It limited the light in our hall, and the process of building was noisy. Relations between us and the builder were somewhat strained.

One day his wife came to our door to pass on some message or other. The door was glass, and she looked down in contempt and laughed at my bare feet on the marble floor.

"You've got no shoes on . . ." she sneered. I was meant to look ashamed, and this was supposed to give her the upper hand. It was a subtle form of bullying. I didn't play her game though. I looked her steadily in the eyes and said: "So what?"

She cringed. While this was not a particularly important fight, those words sum up an attitude in life. If you go with the so-what factor, it gives you a certain invincibility. Be shameless about everything every time. If someone sneers at the state of your clothes, go with the moment. Wear your cat hair with pride. Tell the interesting story of just how you got the hole in your trousers, or whatever else is wrong.

The so-what factor has accompanied me through my literary career. I do not sweep my multiple rejections under the carpet. They are a part of the picture. And quite a few of my poems were triggered by minor humiliations. The sexual snubs etcetera became great copy, and I got paid for them. I had the last laugh.

Another one of those so-what moments came when I was living in an ex-pat ghetto in Spain and the Brits were trying to bully us out. The little man who had told his grandson to stone our cat came to our door, knocked, and said to me: "You think you're better than us, don't you?" Instead of backing down, I gave him my so-what look and said: "Well, my IQ is 50 points higher than yours for starters . . ."

Soon after that, we were able to move away.

Canoe

JAMIE SPRIGGS

In the late afternoon, whenever I have the chance, I go out on the lake.

I scoop up my little dog in one arm, hold on to my ancient Old Town canoe with the other, and scramble down the embankment into the water. The canoe goes down first, then Cassis is carefully deposited within, and at last I ease myself onto a seat and set out for a paddle.

I enjoy everything about the lake: the light reflecting off the water's surface; the lake weed striving toward the sun, stretching long and thin from the sandy bottom to the surface; the rich smell of life in all its stages that sits heavy in the air. I love the water bugs that crawl up onto lily pads before becoming dragonflies, and I love the dragonflies themselves, their small bursts of improbable blues and golds and teals and metallic greens with translucent wings. There are cormorants and geese and ducks and swans, and I love them all.

But what I seek in the golden late-afternoon light is the great blue heron that likes to fish just before evening falls in the shade of an island.

As I paddle the canoe from the shore to the island, I quiet as much as possible so as not to disturb the heron, which I admire from afar. Generally, we sit this way contentedly for quite a while, my little dog and I: She luxuriates in ear scritches, while I drink in the beauty that surrounds us.

One afternoon we had sat quietly long enough to fool the denizens of the lake, and a muskrat surfaced only inches from the side of the canoe.

She was not expecting us. She startled, jumping up and quickly diving back under the water. My little dog startled, barking at the diving muskrat and the churning water she left in her wake. The heron startled and flew off, leaving me alone in my rocking canoe with an agitated dog and the bubbles left behind by the departing wildlife.

I was filled with joy at the experience, delighted for the muskrat and the heron and my little dog and the beauty of it all, and I was suffused with gratitude.

The very next day, as I have a habit of doing when I am able, I once again pulled my canoe into the lake and brought my little dog for a paddle, seeking the company of the heron that likes to fish before the evening falls.

Once again I stilled, approaching the fishing ground; once again we sat quiet on the surface of the lake.

But on that day no muskrat surfaced—instead, a jet ski roared by, disturbing the lake, unsettling the heron. As my little dog barked and the canoe rocked, I thought angry thoughts in the direction of the operator, ticking off in my head the town regulations he was violating: moving too quickly, too close to shore, in too shallow water. I was not full of gratitude.

We were in no physical danger, but the heron was disturbed, along with the local geese and swans. For the rest of the paddle, I told myself the story of how he wrecked my paddle that day with his selfish disregard for both neighbor and nature.

Except, of course, he did nothing of the sort. That jet-skier may very well have been in violation of a handful of regulations, and most certainly was oblivious to his effect on herons and other waterfowl, but I wrecked my own paddle that day. Just as my love for the muskrat had filled me with gratitude, my aversion to the jet ski filled me with all the wrong things, and in my self-righteousness I clung to them and repeated them and made myself miserable.

Sometimes it seems I have spent a lifetime holding on to anger that only hurts me, and does no good for anyone else. The jet-skiers of the world remain unaffected by my emotions. It does not matter if I am right; I would rather be wise.

It is still true that in the late afternoon, whenever I have the chance, I go out on the lake to seek the great blue heron that fishes in the shade of the island before the evening falls.

But perhaps, just perhaps, I have learned to hold things a little more lightly. Perhaps age does bring wisdom.

And I am full of gratitude.

The Bark Test

TRACY STRAUSS

A dog is a (wo)man's best friend, though for most of my life I had no evidence to prove it. Until my mid-forties, I'd only had cats as companions. While mine were loving creatures who snuggled by my side, they scratched and bit me when they were dissatisfied, and, when I went away for a weekend, upon my return they snubbed their noses at me for an equal amount of time.

When I adopted my first dog, Beau, a part-Labrador retriever, part-hound puppy, I was forty-six and living alone, a single woman in the middle of the coronavirus pandemic. Dating seemed near impossible in social isolation, but I had to keep living somehow, so I swiped through the apps and agreed to a phone call or a video chat if the guy seemed half-decent. Unfortunately, things generally fizzled after that, since meeting in person for a date had potentially life-or-death consequences, and the chance of a true partnership needed to be quite high before either of us seemed willing to take the risk. However, I'd never been good at assessing the promise of a potential mate over the phone. Eventually, I grew frustrated by the weeks and months of aloneness and suggested a social distance walk as a first meeting—as long as the guy was agreeable to my bringing along Beau, who had separation anxiety and couldn't be left at home.

I thought the hound part of Beau might sniff out Mr. Right. I planned the path we'd take around Harvard Square, in the hopes we'd avoid any skateboarders or small running kids or people on Rollerblades, all of which suddenly turned a rather sweet and obedient Beau into what I can only describe as the Tasmanian Devil in one of his spinning fits on the *Bugs Bunny* cartoon series. Once, while on a social distance walk with a friend, a surprise skateboarder caused Beau to react so quickly that I crashed to the pavement, bloodying my hands and knees.

When we met Jason, a forty-seven-year-old sales rep whose profile was posted on Bumble with a photo of himself with a dog (he later confessed the dog wasn't his), Beau jumped up to greet him. "Oh, hello!" said Jason, leaning back, laughing nervously.

"Beau," I said, "sit."

Beau ignored me. I pulled him off Jason.

"That's okay," Jason said. "I love dogs."

We walked and conversed about Jason's job at the local grocery store, his ex, his apartment . . . his everything. I can't say I was interested in pursuing a relationship, but the company wasn't unpleasant, even if that was setting a low bar. While we walked my preordained route, Beau sniffed at grassy patches and tree stumps in an uncharacteristically hyper manner, picking up junk that I'd trained him to leave.

I couldn't speak a full sentence to Jason without interrupting myself with "Beau, no," or redirecting him with a treat. Every so often he'd suddenly leap up at Jason's face, his tongue hanging out, causing Jason to take a few steps back.

"I'm so sorry!" I said.

"That's okay," Jason repeated. "I love dogs."

Then Beau crouched at the edge of the city sidewalk and had a bout of diarrhea. He didn't poop in one place, but moved around with every splat. Cleaning up dog diarrhea is a near-impossible feat on pavement; at least if it's done on a patch of dirt, one can use the earth to help gather and soak it up. Generally, dog diarrhea is just dog diarrhea, but as I bent down to clean up the mess, feeling as if I was finger painting the ground with a poop bag as my brush, I wondered if Beau was sending a message to me about Jason, who stood nearby, awkwardly looking, then not looking.

After an hour, Jason and I parted ways. I expected Beau to react in the way he did the first time (and every time after) he met my friends, my family, and my therapist: barking fiercely and lunging in their direction, trying to prevent them from leaving. With Jason, Beau stood quietly, watching him go.

"He's not the one," I said.

I turned, and Beau followed. We walked to the car.

Beau is the kind of best friend who will tell it to me straight, which sometimes means through his behavior, gastrointestinal and otherwise. But if, by chance, I haven't gleaned the full picture, each date culminates in the Beau test: I await his bark.

Senior Project

MIRANDA WRIGHT

How are you supposed to feel a week before graduation? The question has come to me at 2:00 a.m. as I lie on my bed in the same clothes I've had on for three days now, hair unwashed, buzzing on caffeine—feeling desperate. Maybe that's not a normal state to be in a week before graduation, but I've never been great at normal. That's probably how I ended up at art school in the first place.

I'm sure some of you are thinking that my feelings of desperation are to be expected from someone graduating with a BFA—that it's probably just dawned on me how bleak my job prospects are and stuff like that. But that's not it. Not for me, tonight.

Let's start at the beginning.

I chose art school against nearly everyone's *strong* advice. In our material world, it's not really the most rational of degrees—I get that. Most art students don't start out with Polonius's clever advice to his son, Laertes, as he was departing for school in *Hamlet*. I'm sure if Laertes had opted for art school, Polonius's advice would have been more like—*And don't come crawling back to me when you're broke!*

Nevertheless . . . I take each man's censure while reserving my judgment, though no one has advised me, above all else, to mine own self be true.

And there never seems to be any shortage of censure.

As a student of art, I continually brush off disappointed head shakes from my parents' acquaintances as if it were second nature. I ignore comments like *It's not too late to think about law school*. I take in the pitiful smiles that are always followed up with an uncomfortable *How nice for you*, as if I had just proudly announced I was getting early parole.

And of my work, my personal favorite line is: *My six-year-old could do this*.

If not all this, then what's with the desperation, you may ask. My *real* worry tonight is the project I have yet to finish in order to graduate. The

Senior Project, besides being the way to show everyone what you're really passionate about, is also material proof that we have actually learned something in the last four years. As a visual artist who also identifies as a writer, I included a combination of these two disciplines in my project. In semesters past, I was able to get some positive feedback on a mock-up two-page spread for a children's book. All I had to do was multiply that by sixteen and I would be done! Simple, right? Maybe Michelangelo thought the same thing looking up at the whitewashed ceiling of the Sistine Chapel: "Just keep adding to it, and soon you'll be finished." Probably not.

Did Michelangelo know more about children? Probably. Why did I ever feel like I had something to say to them, and in *rhyme* for God's sake! I don't speak in sonnets; I don't even think in a remotely structured form.

Undaunted, a picture book is what I continued to do. *Pat the Bunny* and *Paddington Bear* were the ones who had a seminal formation in my critical examination of the universe. They were among the characters that introduced me to my passion for storytelling.

I had a couple false starts in that department. My touch-and-feel version of *Oedipus Rex* seemed promising at first, but ran into problems with the mother/wife thing—and that really is the best part. Keeping with the redemption theme, I tried playing with a dumbed-down version of Dante's journey through the *Circles of the Inferno* for an epic poetry meets a learn-your-numbers kinda thing. Lots of problems there I probably should have foreseen.

False starts and unusually nice spring weather have left me here tonight, fretting about how much work I have left to do. However, fear not, for *if it be not now, yet it will come.* And that time has come (or it will in the morning). I will finish *Do Ducks Know It's Monday*—my own addition to the world of epistemological inquiry.

On an unrelated note, if you are an underclass art student—ENJOY THESE LAST BLISSFUL MOMENTS OF FREEDOM! IN THAT FREEDOM FIND WHO YOU REALLY ARE AND HOLD ONTO THAT FOR DEAR LIFE! IT GETS HARDER TO DO LATER ON!!!

That wasn't screaming. That was enthusiasm.

Second Acts, Or My Year of 50

SHEREE R. MARCUCCI

My second act was borne out of a dark place.

The year 2005, which is when I turned fifty, was the year I racked up most of the experiences defined as "major life stressors."

Don't worry; it's years later, and you'll see I'm here and thriving.

In November 2004 I was planning an eightieth birthday celebration for my mom. But an initially innocuous injury to her ankle in April 2005 set off a series of infections, and due to her allergic reaction to potent antibiotics, she was just too weak and unable to fight off the infection now lodged in her heart. She said she was ready to face her Lord and consented to having the life support removed.

After her death I was orphaned; my family-of-origin members were all gone.

As I grieved my mother and returned to my routine, I suddenly had to deal with my own injury. After exiting a municipal building on a beautiful May day, I unexpectedly fell soundly on my bottom. The colleague with whom I was walking helped me get quickly to my feet and back to work.

The next day I awoke to excruciating neck pain. During the course of the fall I'd experienced whiplash, much as if I'd been in a car accident. Much later, I could feel, in addition to the injury, the fury I experienced after reading the doctor's callous remarks, reprinted in the lawsuit I filed: "Patient overwrought and extremely upset." I was in unbearable pain and in deep grief. How did he think I should feel?

By early August, I was determined to mark my fiftieth year in style, although I hadn't met all the goals I'd set for myself by that time. But I had, for example, quit smoking two years before—a genuine accomplishment. I'd also come to terms with the fact that I was going through menopause, recognizing my body's transition with both relief and a little bit of loss. I felt as I if I could fully embrace being the Birthday Queen, and so, with friends, I did.

By late August, however, I began to sink into what I now know was depression.

My oldest son went off to college, which we also celebrated. By September, I knew he was struggling, not academically but in much the same way I was—emotionally.

I knew I needed to help him, but how? He was legally an adult. Because of an intervention by an insightful APRN, he received the help he needed.

Now I have decided that God was guiding us through the process, but when you're in the middle of the storm, you don't see the spiritual weather map.

Just in case that doesn't seem like enough, in 2005 I was entering a new phase of life professionally as well. After working happily for seventeen years at one place, I was no longer in alignment with the leadership and knew I needed to make a change.

I began to put feelers out. It's hard to face change, even when it's what you want and it's for the better.

By October I had taken a new job: I held a leadership position with a not-for-profit performing arts venue.

Remember when I mentioned the things I went through in 2005 scored high on life stressor assessment scales? By my count I'd gone through eight in ten months.

But the experience that almost broke me, oddly enough, wasn't about mortality, or aging, or loss. It had to do with getting (almost) exactly what I wanted and beginning a new career in the world of professional theater. My dream job brought me to lows I hadn't ever before imagined. Why? Because my overriding fear was the very deep worry that I was in way over my head. Would I still be able to swim?

I'd always relied on my skills, my smarts, and my wits.

Yet I would begin each workday in a panic crying, telling my husband I couldn't do this. Yet still, each day I pulled on my big girl pants and made it through.

Like an infant, I learned to crawl, walk, then at times run with the joy of getting past my old demons, leaving them behind.

There is nothing in 2005 I would now change. I learned from every moment.

I've decided that second acts can have the most triumphal arcs: Out of the darkness can come a new light and a clarity of vision.

The Bridge Ladies

BONNIE JEAN FELDKAMP

On my third day as the community center's new executive director, I introduced myself to The Bridge Ladies.

"Do you play bridge?" One lady asked. "We're one short, and Gayle would sit in when we were short."

I had replaced Gayle.

"I'm sorry, um . . . your name?" I asked the spokesperson. Her face tightened. She was their ringleader. I apparently had no valid reason to know her name.

"I'm sorry, ma'am," I said, "playing cards would be a misuse of my time."

"Then could you call someone to fill the spot?" she asked. "Gayle kept a file."

When I arrived earlier that morning, I discovered that someone had emptied the contents of all the files into the bottom drawer of the file cabinet. Did she know? Or did she just know that without knowing anyone's name, that list—once I found it—was useless?

These were Gayle's friends. During my interview, the hiring board let me know that Gayle had "used the center like her own clubhouse." I would have to win over some of the regulars. These ladies *had* to give me a hard time if they wanted to save face with their fired friend.

I had worried that being an outsider would work against me. But now, I knew hiring an outsider was imperative. I had moved from Cincinnati, Ohio, to west Michigan. The community center was in the small, affluent, aptly-named town of Richland.

I found Donna, the center's custodian, in the kitchen cleaning the coffeepot while one of The Bridge Ladies sat at my desk looking through the phone book.

"Who supplies their snacks?" I asked.

"We do," Donna said. "Gayle always bought 'em."

The next time The Bridge Ladies gathered to play, I stocked a cart with snacks. I also placed a cup on the cart with a label on it that read "Donations."

"There's no lemonade," someone said.

"We don't have any lemonade," I responded and showed the ladies the donation cup.

"I can continue to shop for your snacks using any money put in the donation cup as your budget." I smiled and tried to sound optimistic.

"I pay my taxes," someone challenged.

"The community center is a nonprofit organization. We do not receive tax monies," I explained.

"I know the center has a benefactress," the ringleader said. Her arms crossed over her chest.

"The endowment covers our cost of operations, that's true," I said, "but programs and activities are expected to be self-sustaining." I tried to explain the situation gently but was losing my patience.

"Gayle always took care of our snacks," said the ringleader.

My frustration flared. "And that is one of the reasons she is no longer here."

The ringleader's lips parted, but she caught herself before her jaw could completely drop.

Later, when Donna wheeled the cart of dishes into the kitchen, I took the donation cup and counted 37 cents. Mostly pennies. I was glad the ladies liked Donna. Otherwise, I think she would have found those pennies in the bottom of half-full cups of coffee.

When I cleaned out the file cabinet, I found a copy of a letter to the board with a signed petition attached. The letter protested Gayle's dismissal. There had been a community-wide attempt to keep her as executive director.

The next day one of The Bridge Ladies walked into my office and donated a large tin of coffee. She leaned in and lowered her voice. "Don't let Linda get to you. It's just that Gayle's her best friend."

So the ringleader's name was Linda.

"I really hope that Gayle will rejoin the group someday," I said. "She's welcome here. It's her community center too." I meant it.

The next week I wheeled the cart of snacks into the room and told the ladies there had been an anonymous donation of coffee but the snack stash was dwindling.

At the end of the day, I counted $4.89 and was able to buy a dozen chocolate chip cookies on sale in the supermarket bakery. As the snack quality increased, so did the donations and the morale. Even Linda eventually smiled and said "Good morning" when I wheeled in the snack cart.

It took Gayle almost a year to come back, but she did. The board was right to hire an outsider. I hoped with the stress of running the community center gone, she could really enjoy the place with her friends for what it was—hers.

Thin Ice

BARBARA COOLEY

My footsteps drummed their determined rhythm on the polished, hard vinyl floor. The final stretch in my nearly mile-long hike from the parking structure into the main building and on through to the East Wing was one long expanse of glass-like surface, reminiscent of the small neighborhood ice rink next to our childhood home. He and I would be out there all day until called home, gliding silently around the smooth, frozen surface, the only sound the slice of our blades as we pushed forward. Always pushing forward, just like I was pushing forward down the hall.

I'd have rather been skating and so would he, but in those early days I began to appreciate the value of military marches, each step calling my brain to attention with its repetitive beat, drowning out extraneous thoughts, focusing inward, laser-like, on my only goal—my mission. I settled into the stride of my own steps, the echo of them ricocheting off the walls, the sound and sensation merging into one single-minded thought: to get back to my brother, to keep him alive.

Drawing closer to his room, I stepped lighter, softer, in case he was sleeping. The toxic buildup in his brain had begun to transform sounds, and footsteps might become the rhythmic drumbeat of an indigenous population—not threatening, merely distracting and disconcerting as he would try to orient himself to time and place. Africa? The north woods? Never the last room on the South Unit of the East Wing's eighth floor. One by one, his vital organs were struggling, then failing, causing toxic buildups throughout his body, ultimately manifesting in his mental state. Uncommunicative at times, adopting a façade of equanimity at others, he fought to appear normal and in control. But his comments and questions revealed the chaos he was experiencing physically, mentally, and emotionally.

One morning he complained bitterly that he had hardly slept at all, as ". . . the kids were doing belly slides down the hall all night." "What kids?" I asked, and he replied, "You know; *the kids*." "What are belly slides?" I wondered aloud, and his disdainful response told me I should have known they were when you flopped down on your belly and slid across the floor. Most nights I had taken to sleeping in his room with him, stretched out on a chair that extended flat into a single-size bed. I didn't sleep so much as doze, listening for sounds of his breathing, his restlessness causing mine.

One night around 3:00 a.m., his increased thrashing about told me he was awake, so I whispered, "Can't sleep?" "What are we doing in the Schmidts' living room?" he asked, puzzled. My instinct to orient him caused me to correct him. "We're not in the Schmidts' living room. We're in Beaumont Hospital in Royal Oak." His agitated response of "No. We're in the Schmidts' living room!" conveyed his need to have his perceptions affirmed, so I responded, "I don't know what we're doing here. I've never been in their living room before. Is this the old house or their new one?" The Schmidts had lived down the street from us fifty years earlier; their kids were our classmates.

That night we walked through our old neighborhood, dropping in on neighbors, describing their houses, their families, their backyard barbecues or pools, the big color TVs, and we detailed some of our exploits, both the typical ones and those that could have been harbingers of a delinquent path. We marveled over how fast we ran after ringing neighbors' doorbells then hiding in bushes. We recalled the night he and his friends had hung the neighbor's wooden hobby horse in a tree. We slipped out of our shoes and into our ice skates for a long, smooth glide on the rink. After visiting with families from our youth, Don settled down and drifted off to sleep, assured that we were in the right place and time, the same place and time, walking together down the old street, skating silently on the old rink.

He hovered between life and death—between this world and some foggy other world—for weeks, but later he told me he heard my footsteps coming down the hall. He knew they weren't the kids doing belly slides or the indigenous people drumming. They were the footsteps of his sister marching to fight for him, to skate with him, to help his blades slice the thin ice and keep him pushing forward.

Put a Smile on Your Face

YVONNE RANSEL

"Put a smile on your face and no one will notice what you're wearing," my father would say when I moaned about my sad adolescent wardrobe. I adored my Italian high school–educated philosopher, so I took what he said to heart. I was happy; I was sort of popular; I had nice dark hair and eyes.

So I smiled a lot, for years—until I couldn't.

It was 1983, and I spent my days substitute teaching and carpooling two kids around almost daily to after-school sporting or music events. When an astute ENT was suspicious of my sudden one-sided hearing loss, he suggested a brain scan. I thought I was humoring him by agreeing to it, but no one was laughing when the word "tumor" arose.

An acoustic neuroma it was called. And I couldn't even Google it back then. Before brain scans, these benign but dangerous tumors weren't even identified in time to not cause harm. I frantically "interviewed" three local ENTs who had only performed a handful of these brain surgeries and found, in relief, a doctor who had done hundreds and had trained with the best.

Little did I know that the ten-hour surgery, three hours from home, would be the easy part of the long recovery process. For over a month I was housebound, and dear friends would come and take me for rides to see the October leaves or stay and teach me how to play cribbage or leave food— and books.

I would sit in the front seat of our converted van and clap when my son scored a goal—the clap I only half heard, because to remove the tumor, my auditory, balance, and facial nerves had to be severed. The entire right side of my face drooped, and I lost my smile, the one thing that made up for all my insecurities—in high school, in college, around my husband's country club parents, of moving to a new town, in making new friends.

I was grateful my astute surgeon scheduled a second surgery to amazingly splice the facial nerve to the lingual one. I was only thirty-five, and he knew I had so much more living to do. It took months, but the facial tone began to return, along with my strangely crooked smile. I spent those months trying to return to some sort of normal, but I could feel the puzzled and pitying second looks, which saddened and then empowered me.

I refused to cancel a planned skiing trip and made a few runs, only to realize my balance would likely never improve. I learned to turn my good side to the camera, and my vanity showed when I was caught off-guard. When spring came, I tried in vain to ride my bike and knew, as I aged, I probably never would again.

I dreaded, of all things, my twentieth high school reunion with my new face, but it seemed that no one noticed or were simply happy to see the class secretary. My hair had grown out, thank goodness, after being shaved for the surgery, but it was necessary to color the early gray caused by that trauma. From then on, I was fearless in my endeavors—trial by fire, because . . . why not?

I knew I had skill sets that would override my severed nerves. I took the next five years to get my masters in Library Science and worked in college, state, and public libraries; I opened a bar and restaurant to pay homage to my mother's Italian cooking after she died; I made great friends in the local music scene by hiring blues and jazz bands weekly to entertain my eclectic clientele; I got political and managed a couple local campaigns; I played tennis until the ortho said "no no." I still play bad golf; I paint and I write.

And then, the other day, I watched a YouTube video of a Zoom writing class I recently gave to a retirement community here in Florida. I had never seen myself speaking. I stared at my mouth that didn't quite move right and my right eye that kept closing on its own.

I asked my husband in horror, "Is that what I look like when I talk? Is that my weirdly lispy voice?" He didn't answer me, and I realized that all these years, my crooked smile was good enough and it was my father's voice that carried me here.

Living in the Moment

TERI RIZVI

"It's just about the moments. That's all life really is," my friend Jim said quietly over the phone after breaking the news that he had been diagnosed with inoperable lung cancer.

I have known no one better than Jim at living in the moment. Most of us are too busy choreographing the future.

I flashed back to 1979 as Jim and my college roommates, Toni and Denise, belted out—complete with synchronized hand gestures—"Stop in the Name of Love" in our living room.

After graduation, Denise's camera captured us outside a London tube station, surrounded by a mountain of luggage and an avalanche of apprehension. This was the start of a post-college adventure decided on impulse late one night at the kitchen table. As the only one who had stepped foot in England before, Jim helped orient us before heading to Amsterdam for an internship with the Associated Press while I stayed to work for McGraw-Hill World News.

After returning home, we surprised our parents with the news that we were flying back across the Atlantic again—without jobs this time. We had talked each other into taking a chance on newfound loves. I eventually married mine.

When Jim told me he was dying, I yearned to sit down at the computer keyboard to tease from my heart all the right words. Instead, I bought an airline ticket to New York City.

After checking into a nearby hotel, I walked down East 17th Street to Jim's walk-up Chelsea apartment. The wail of sirens punctuated the cool March air, and I instinctively quickened my pace.

As I climbed four flights, I girded myself. Looking wan, weary, and rail-thin, he greeted me with a welcoming smile and an apology: "I'm not much of a host these days." The walls of his comfortable, cozy studio featured bright, bold abstract paintings by his former lover, and the bookshelves overflowed with dog-eared books and CDs, including every Patsy Cline recording ever made. He had propped open a screenless window, but a musty smell lingered, a harbinger of life slipping slowly away.

We sorted through faded issues of the *Butler Aviator*, the high school newspaper we edited, and fondly recalled our principal, who excused us from some classes after we told him we took home "midnight oil pages" to proof. While our peers were stuck in Civics, we ran to the printer and skipped cafeteria food for tastier lunches and long conversations at a tiny café in a nearby town. Was it ink in the blood or the joy of newfound freedom that drew us to journalism?

For me, that call may have gone unanswered without Jim's insistence that I transfer from community college to journalism school. I enrolled at Ohio University, sight unseen, with few funds and little faith in myself.

A gifted writer, Jim was named editor of *The Post*, the daily student newspaper, and gave me the managing editor's role. We spent our days chasing stories and our nights singing along to Frankie Valli and the Four Seasons and Slim Whitman tunes in those slaphappy predawn hours spent putting the paper to bed.

Decades later, as Jim lies on the couch tethered to oxygen, we eat bagels, chat about everything and nothing, and listen to Lesley Gore croon "You Don't Own Me" and "It's My Party (I'll Cry If I Want To)." There were no tears, only the words you speak when you worry you won't get another chance.

I thanked him for helping me believe in myself at a vulnerable time in my life, for writing the treasured box of letters stored in the attic, for sharing homespun short stories for my editing eye—and for amusing me with the way he saw the world.

It's not often a friend uses "exquisite," "sultry," and "sublime" all in the same sentence, but that's how he mourned his musical icon Peggy Lee in one of his more unforgettable emails.

Later that evening—his last at home before I made the heartbreaking call to Hospice—his close friends, Jim and Dan, come over, and we laugh and reminisce about music and literature and travels. At one point, despite his growing weakness, Jim bursts into a refrain from a Peggy Lee song.

As we listen in amazement, I understand with full force the lesson he taught me: "It's just about the moments."

Contributors

Angela Aisevbonaye is a graduate student with the University of Connecticut's Department of Public Policy. She has a fondness for spoonerisms, portmanteaus, astonishing feats of alliteration, and other curiosities in wordplay. A longtime singer and songwriter, she sometimes giddily bursts into song at random, often making up lyrics on the fly. On any given weekend, she can be found reading, ensconced in a jam session, or luxuriating in the shower, beatifically deep-conditioning the glorious little coils that sprout from her head. Though, if you happen to find her in the shower, kindly let her be. At least let her get her bantu knots started.

Anne Bagamery is a journalist based in Paris. She grew up in the Detroit suburbs and graduated in 1978 from Dartmouth, where she was the first woman editor-in-chief of *The Dartmouth* campus daily. A former senior editor of the late, lamented *International Herald Tribune* in Paris, her work has appeared in *Forbes*, *Institutional Investor*, *Savvy*, *Worth*, the *International New York Times*, the *American Lawyer*, *Persuasion*, and Vogue. com.

Courtney Baklik, author of "Please Do Not Enter When the Door Is Locked: A Guide to Pumping at Work," is a high school English teacher but considers parenting her two toddlers her real job. She completed her undergraduate degree

as well as two master's degrees at the University of Connecticut, which is, more importantly, where she studied writing with Gina Barreca. Courtney has lived and worked her entire life in Connecticut and appreciates the comfort and community of the small towns that hold special places in her heart.

Louisa Ballhaus is an NYC-based writer and editor with work in Betches, Bustle, SheKnows, and Merry Jane. She's worked on HBO Max's *Search Party* and was the poetry editor for literary magazine *2 Bridges Review*. Her poetry has appeared in *Free State Review*, and she earned her BA in English from Wesleyan University.

Dr. Hannah Ballou is a comedian, performance artist, writer, and lecturer at Kingston University, London. Her first film, *goo:ga II*, will be released in 2021. Recent performance work includes "Shhh," "hoo:ha," "goo:ga," "Lambchop Magoo Does Brexit," and "The Doctor Is In." She has written for McSweeney's and Comedy Studies. She is also known for her cabaret persona, Lambchop Magoo, and the Marina Abramopug Project.

Gina Barreca, Board of Trustees Distinguished Professor of English at the University of Connecticut, has written ten books, including the best-selling *They Used to Call Me Snow White, But I Drifted* and *Babes in Boyland: A Personal History of Coeducation in the Ivy League*; and edited seventeen others, including *Fast Funny Women: 75 Essays of Flash Nonfiction*. Translated into Chinese, Japanese, German, and Spanish, her scholarly and trade books have helped establish the study of women's humor as a Thing. Barreca's essays have been published by the *New York Times*, the *Independent of London*, *Cosmopolitan*, and the *Harvard Business Review*. Gina's *Psychology Today* blog has well over seven million views. She has no hobbies (and yet can be counted on to bring the party with her).

Originally from Chicago, **Pia Bertucci** relocated to the Carolinas to pursue a doctorate in Italian from the University of North Carolina at Chapel Hill. Currently, she is the Director of Italian at the University of South Carolina. In addition to her 2015 novel, *Between Milk and India,* Pia has published on Italian women writers, Italian food studies, and the Italian language. When she's not working, Pia can be found eating her way through Italy, soaking in Colorado hot springs, attending Toad the Wet Sprocket concerts, or enjoying time with her husband, four children, and two dogs.

Beth Blatt's musicals, plays, and songs have been performed at the Kennedy Center, the UN, Lincoln Center, across the United States, Asia, and Europe. Her work has garnered an array of highly respected awards, grants, fellowships, and residencies. Her musical *The Mistress Cycle* was produced in New York, London, twice in Chicago; and *Island of the Blue Dolphins* (TheatreWorks USA) toured the United States. Her play, *In Her Words,* has been seen in and near New York City. She is founder of Hope Sings, whose mission is to harness the power of song/story to support women. Songs include "One Woman," the anthem for UN women. Visit her at www.bethblatt.com and www.hopesings.net

An award-winning expert in applied democracy, consultant **Nancy Bocskor** has worked in twenty-eight countries and all fifty states, preparing women for leadership roles in politics and public service. Most recently, she served as the interim Executive Director of the Public Leadership Education Network (PLEN), a nationwide organization that trains college women for public policy positions in government, corporations, and associations.
Tagged a "Democracy Coach" by *Die Welt,* a major German newspaper, Bocskor "spreads democracy throughout the world. . . . The lively American travels from one country to the next coaching candidates on how to win elections, especially encouraging women to make it into parliament."

Patricia Wynn Brown is an award-winning writer and performer. She has published two books, performed her humor memoir one-woman show, *Hair Theater Beauty School*, across the country for fifteen years, and is a frequent speaker. Unamused by Patricia's classroom comedy antics, her high school teaching nun, Sister Consilia, announced that she would end up in a women's prison. She did, but it is to do volunteer projects there, and Warden Baldauf allows her exit.

Laura Caparrotti is a director, actress, journalist, teacher, lecturer, consultant, dialect coach, and curator with an Italian accent. She has studied and worked professionally for over ten years in Italy before relocating to New York. She is the Founding Artistic Director of KIT-Kairos Italy Theater, the main Italian Theater Company in New York. In 2013 Laura started In Scena! Italian Theater Festival NY, the first Italian theater festival to take place in all five New York boroughs and beyond. In 2019 she inaugurated On Stage!, the first American theater festival in Italy as associate director.

Ashaliegh Carrington is a freelance writer who recently graduated from the University of Connecticut with a double major in English and History. She has been published by Long Wharf Theatre, the Teagle Foundation, and Honeysuckle Media. Her work ranges from writing short stories to focusing on local journalism. She is excited to be included among other hardworking women who are not afraid to tell their stories.

Nicole Catarino is a senior at the University of Connecticut, pursuing a BA in English with a concentration in Creative Writing. Her writing has appeared in the *Hartford Courant*, and she was both a contributor and an editor for the first book in this flash nonfiction anthology, *Fast Funny Women*. In the past, she has also served as the Interviews Editor and as a fiction panelist for the *Long River Review* literary journal. On any given day, you can find her drinking boba tea and listening to her extensive collection of Spotify playlists.

Mary Ann Caws is the editor of the *Yale Anthology of Twentieth-Century French Poetry*, the *HarperCollins World Literature*, *Milk-Bowl of Feathers*, *The Surrealist Painters and Poets*, and *Surrealist Love Poetry*; author of *Creative Gatherings: Meeting Places of Modernism*, the *Modern Art Cook Book*, *To the Boathouse*, *Glorious Eccentrics*; and translator of Tristan Tzara's *Approximate Man and Other Writings*, André Breton's *Mad Love*, and Jacques Derrida and Paule Thévenin's *The Secret Art of Antonin Artaud*. She is an Officier of the Palmes Académiques; a Chevalier dans l'ordre des Arts et des Lettres; the recipient of Guggenheim, Rockefeller, and Getty fellowships; and a fellow of the American Academy of Arts and Sciences.

Lisa Chau is the author of *Small Talk Techniques: Smart Strategies for Personal and Professional Success*. She founded Clover Canal to guide international clients in content creation, digital strategy, and the development of compelling narratives to showcase professional leadership. Her writing has been published more than 130 times in *Forbes*, *Buzzfeed*, *Thrive Global*, *US News & World Report*, as well as *Huffington Post* on TABLES: Technology–Academia–Business–Leadership–Entrepreneurship–Strategy. In addition to speaking at multiple Ivy League campuses, including Yale, Princeton, and her alma mater, Dartmouth College, Lisa has been a Ted-Ed lesson creator and guest on NPR. https://CloverCanal2020.wordpress.com

Catherine Conant has enjoyed a long career as an oral storyteller, story coach, and writer. She has appeared throughout the country at schools, corporate settings, and storytelling festivals. Her writing includes a humor column, essays, and *Learning Through Living Histories*, a story project in which fifth-grade students interviewed and wrote the stories of military veterans. A longtime Connecticut resident, she recently relocated to Phoenix, Arizona, where the winters are mild but there is a shocking lack of oceanfront property. She can be contacted at catherinecconant@gmail.com.

Jane Cook is a lifelong learner and educator. She has worked in K–12 education for more than forty years and has worked part-time with the Connecticut Writing Project at the University of Connecticut since 2007. When not working, Jane spends her time rescuing animals (twenty-five cats and dogs and one horse), paying vet bills, and standing up to bosses. She started writing in high school, for her high school newspaper, and hasn't stopped since. Jane lives in Mansfield Center, Connecticut, with her husband, Chip Gough, and her current animal family members: Zen, Willow, Joy, and Ami.

Have laptop, will write. **Barbara Cooley** is a former college instructor and nonprofit administrator and consultant who now writes for the sheer pleasure of it. Her current projects include the story of her brother's fierce battle with leukemia and an epic narrative detailing five generations of one line in her family that mirrors the story of America. She lives in her happy place along the Lake Michigan shoreline with her husband and her rescue dog, who believes *he* is her only laptop. Her other talents of note include welding and parallel parking, although she doesn't boast about the welding.

Maureen Corrigan, book critic for NPR's *Fresh Air*, is the Nicky and Jamie Grant Distinguished Professor of the Practice in Literary Criticism  at Georgetown University. She is an associate editor of and contributor to *Mystery and Suspense Writers* (Scribner) and was the winner of the 1999 Edgar Award for Criticism, presented by the Mystery Writers of America. In 2019 Corrigan was awarded the Nona Balakian Citation for Excellence in Reviewing by the National Book Critics Circle. Corrigan served as a juror for the 2012 Pulitzer Prize in Fiction. Her book *So We Read On: How the Great Gatsby Came to Be and Why It Endures* was published by Little, Brown and Company in September 2014. Corrigan's literary memoir *Leave Me Alone, I'm Reading!* was published in 2005. Corrigan is also a reviewer and columnist for the *Washington Post* Book World, and she has chaired the Mystery and Suspense judges' panel of the *Los Angeles Times* Book Prize.

Georgia Court has mostly enjoyed a career in words, although she took a detour into high-tech, working a few years as an IBM systems engineer. After earning her master's in Journalism, she was marketing director for a PBS station,  then ran her own PR-events company, wrote a book about event planning, published a health-care newspaper, wrote a regular column for one of Cincinnati's daily newspapers, and taught at the University of Cincinnati. Her latest work adventure: owning Bookstore1 Sarasota, which she opened in March 2011.

Nicole Decker-Lawler is a high school veterinary science teacher in Connecticut. She has been a youth educator since 2008. Nicole attended the University of Connecticut and earned a BA in Communication Sciences with an English minor, a BS in Agriculture and Natural Resources, and an MA in Education. Nicole's passion trifecta includes animals, teaching, and travel! Her current job allows her to blend all three interests together. She organizes trips for her students to travel the world to explore global agriculture. Nicole and her family enjoy their lakeside life in Sandy Hook, Connecticut.

Maria DeCotis is a NYC-based comedian, actress, and writer from Fayetteville, Georgia, where she famously Christmas caroled for Big Boi at age twelve. She graduated with her BFA in Acting, cum laude, from Boston University with a concentration in Playwriting and worked with Commedia dell'Arte professionals in Italy. She has been featured in *Rolling Stone, Vogue, New York* magazine, the *New York Times, Wall Street Journal, The Guardian, New York Daily News, Today,* and many more. Maria's recent credits include opening for Mike Birbiglia on Broadway, Comedy Central, the HBO Women in Comedy Festival, and the New York Comedy Festival.

Alena Dillon is the author of *Mercy House,* a Library Journal Best Book of 2020, optioned as a television series produced by Amy Schumer; *The Happiest Girl in the World,* a *Good Morning America* pick; *My Body Is a Big Fat Temple,* a memoir of pregnancy and early parenting; and a third novel about a woman pilot during WWII and her daughter, forthcoming from William Morrow in fall 2022. Her work has appeared in publications including *LitHub, River Teeth, Slice* magazine, *The Rumpus,* and *Bustle.* She teaches creative writing and lives on the north shore of Boston.

Cindy Eastman is an award winning author whose first book, *Flip-Flops After 50: And Other Thoughts on Aging I Remembered to Write Down*, is a collection of essays on getting older. She is the creator of the Day of Her Own women's writing retreat, and presented nationally at the Story Circle Network Eighth Women's Writing Conference in Austin, Texas. She is a contributor to *Laugh Out Loud: 40 Women Humorists Celebrate Then and Now . . . Before We Forget*,

published in association with the University of Dayton's Erma Bombeck Writers' Workshop. Read additional essays at cindyeastman.com and at various places on the internet.

Niamh Catherine Cunningham Emerson is a communications profes-sional and proud Irish immigrant. Her work has been published in the *Hartford Courant* and two anthologies, *Make Mine a Double: Why Women Like Us Like to Drink* and *Fast Funny Women: 75 Essays of Flash Nonfiction*. She holds a BA in

English and Journalism from the University of Connecticut and an MA in English Language and Literature from Yale University (before you ask, Go Huskies!). In spite of several naysayers at the time, Niamh is even happier now than she was in this picture (taken when she was still Niamh Cunningham), despite changing her name.

Bonnie Jean Feldkamp is the Opinion Editor for the *Louisville Courier-Journal* and a syndicated columnist with Creators Syndicate. She lives with her family in Louisville, Kentucky. Find her on social media @WriterBonnie or at WriterBonnie.com.

Mona Friedland is a New York transplant who abandoned a teaching career for the challenges of the nonprofit sector. There she learned to write grants, proposals, and marketing materials to garner support for various charitable organizations. She was the Executive Director of the Windham Region United Way, Development Director for Hartford's Camp Courant, and Executive Director of the Windham Hospital Foundation. She identifies herself as the happiest retiree ever, continuing to engage in meaningful activities in the community and enjoying her friendships, her family, travel, and the great outdoors.

Jennifer Forrest is a fearless business leader who has a passion for building teams and delivering results. She is on her path to discovering her next chapter. She had the pleasure of being inspired by Gina Barecca while in her writing classes at the University of Connecticut. She lives in Connecticut with her husband and three boys, along with their dogs and bunnies. She is an avid reader and amateur gardener and has a closet full of shoes. This is her first published work.

Rhea Hirshman, a writer, editor, and communications consultant, is also an adjunct professor in the Women's, Gender, and Sexuality Studies Program at the University of Connecticut in Stamford. She has taught at Yale and Wesleyan, has a long history of feminist activism, founded a feminist bookstore in New Haven, and does frequent public speaking. For several years she wrote a gender issues column for the *New Haven Register* and, in an earlier life, was a high school English teacher. As her friends know, she sees no conflict between good politics, good grammar, good works, and a good time.

Polly Ingraham has worked primarily in high schools, both as an English teacher and a school-to-career counselor. She and her husband live in Concord, New Hampshire; their three adult children are elsewhere. In 2018 she completed Grub Street's Memoir Incubator program and continued working to finish her book manuscript. She has attended workshops at the Madeline Island School of the Arts, the New York State Writers Institute, Wesleyan University Writers Conference, and the Iowa Writers Festival. Her work has been published in the *Boston Globe Sunday Magazine*, *Tikkun*, *Dartmouth Alumni Magazine*, and on National Public Radio. Find her blog at www.pastorswifeblog.com.

Nyanka J. is a St. Lucia–born writer. She has published fiction in the *Ponder Review* and the *Caribbean Writer*. Although she enjoys writing fiction, she has written numerous articles critiquing culture and music. Some of her articles can be found in *Okayplayer* and *DJBooth* magazines. When she isn't writing, she can be found looking for the best meal around or binge-watching shows. She aims to tell stories that make black girls feel seen.

Rabbi **Marisa Elana James** is Director of Social Justice Programming at Congregation Beit Simchat Torah, where she oversees the Ark Immigration Clinic, among other holy work. A graduate of the University of Connecticut and the Reconstructionist Rabbinical College, she has been a college English teacher, competitive ballroom dancer, insurance broker, student pilot, and bookstore manager, and has taught Jewish texts and traditions in the United States, Germany, and Israel and Palestine. Marisa and her wife, contrabassoonist and translator Barbara Ann Schmutzler, live (and get into good trouble) in New York City.

Suzy Johnson is a former employee communications consultant, now writing her next chapter in Philadelphia, where she is often seen hanging out at the dog park. She has a BA in English from Kentucky Wesleyan College, an MA from Marquette University, and was pursuing a PhD at the University of Connecticut when she floated her résumé to NYC employers and charted a new path. More recently, she created a popular Twitter account for a panda because . . . pandas. She does not know Elvis, but she knows some Fast Fierce Women, thank goodness.

Pamela Katz is a screenwriter most known for her work with legendary director Margarethe von Trotta, including *Hannah Arendt* (one of *New York Times* critic A. O. Scott's Top Ten Films). As an author, she's published essays and articles, as well as *The Partnership: Brecht, Weill, Three Women and Germany on the Brink*, published by Doubleday/ Nan A. Talese. *The New Yorker* proclaimed: "Katz restores the women to their proper place in the story, with levity, strong characterization, and beguiling descriptions of interwar Germany crackling with politics, art, and a sense of possibility."

Lindsey Keefe has a couple of degrees in English and an entirely unrelated day job. She writes at her sister's old elementary school desk, wedged between two closet doors, and often there's a small human in the background yelling about not wanting to wear underwear. It's the best.

Kim Cochran Kiesewetter lives in North Carolina with her two fierce and fiery daughters and her one overly-loved dog. When not working with libraries as a data analyst and musing about her personal history as a teen mom, she enjoys spending time outside running and kayaking, practicing yoga, and making art.

Sally Koslow is the author of six books, with a seventh coming in 2022 from Harper Collins. Her latest is *Another Side of Paradise*, a bio-novel about F. Scott Fitzgerald's love affair with the truly fierce Sheilah Graham. The former editor-in-chief of *McCall's* and other magazines, Sally has written more than one hundred essays and articles for magazines, newspapers, anthologies, and websites; spoken at the F. Scott Fitzgerald Society in France, colleges, libraries, and synagogues; and has taught at The Writing Institute of Sarah Lawrence College. People often say she's the first person they've met from North Dakota. Visit her at www.sallykoslow.com.

Laurie Laidlaw Deacon has eagerly broadened her writing repertoire with this essay, "May the Fierce Be with You." In it, she speaks of choices, fear, kindness, hope, and insights in a personal and heartwarming story. By day, she is another kind of author, producing lengthy and deeply researched assessments of companies to buy (or not) as a very important person at a very important company. Trained as an attorney, her early-career writing focused on legal briefs, demonstrating for all who read them another finely developed kind of authorship. Laurie's friends would say her handwritten notes are generous, sweet, and meaningful. To her family—husband, two sons, daughters-in-law, and grandchildren—they are notes of love. No one knows what she writes to her silver lab, Remy, since he eats them immediately.

Caroline Leavitt is *The New York Times* best-selling author of twelve novels, including *Pictures of You, Is This Tomorrow, Cruel Beautiful World*, and most recently the *Good Morning America* online pick, *With or Without You*. A New York Foundation of the Arts Fellow, she was a finalist in the Sundance Screenwriters lab. A book critic for *People* and *AARP* magazine and a story structure teacher at UCLA Writers Program Extension online, she runs a column/blog, "Runs in the Family," for *Psychology Today*. Her work has appeared in "Modern Love" in *The New York Times, New York* magazine, *Salon, The Manifest-Station, The Millions, Lit Hub*, and more. Visit her at www.carolineleavitt.com.

Phillis Levin is the author, most recently, of *Mr. Memory & Other Poems* (Penguin, 2016), a finalist for the *Los Angeles Times* Book Prize; her sixth collection is forthcoming. She is the editor of *The Penguin Book of the Sonnet* (2001). Her honors include the Poetry Society of America's Norma Farber First Book Award, a Fulbright Scholar Award to Slovenia, the Amy Lowell Poetry Travelling Scholarship, and fellowships from the Ingram Merrill Foundation, Guggenheim Foundation, and National Endowment for the Arts. She lives in New York City and is a professor of English and poet-in-residence at Hofstra University.

Lia Jill Levitt, MPhil MS CDP, is the founder and CEO of Ain't She Sweet, LLC, a company dedicated to intellectually inspiring seniors. She also owns Academic Architect, LLC, a mentoring-based college and graduate school admissions consultancy. Lia obtained her Master of Philosophy degree from the University of Pennsylvania. She taught at Western Connecticut State University and has guest lectured at Stanford University, University of Connecticut, and

Sacred Heart University. Lia is on the Commission on Aging in Newtown, volunteers with the Alzheimer's Association, and is a Certified Dementia Practitioner. She's published in *Thrive Global, Reader's Digest, Next Avenue*, and other media outlets.

Leighann Lord—back for volume two of *Fast Funny Women*—is a stand-up comedian who's appeared on Comedy Central, HBO, and *The View*. She received the AHA Humanist Arts Award, and her latest comedy specials can be seen on Dry Bar and Showtime. Leighann is the author of several humor books, including *Dict Jokes: Alternate Definitions for Words You've Probably Never Heard of But Will Definitely Never Forget* and *Real Women Do It Standing Up: Stories from the Career of a Very Funny Lady*. She is a former co-host of *StarTalk Radio* with Neil deGrasse Tyson and the creator of the *People with Parents* podcast.

Sheree R. Marcucci has worn many hats during her 2ND ACT—podcast producer, radio host, voice actor, and marketing maven. Her greatest joy has been allowing others to give voice to their own as the creator of 2ND ACT Life Stories and Encore!

Julia Marrinan is from Oakdale, Connecticut, and has been riding horses since before she could walk, for which her mother is to be blamed (or credited, depending on who you ask). She received a bachelor's degree in English and Spanish from the University of Connecticut. If she isn't looking between two equine ears at the next jump, she can be found with her nose in a book at the local library.

A dedicated animal welfare advocate, **Heidi Mastrogiovanni** lives in Los Angeles with her musician husband and their rescued senior dogs. She is a graduate of Wesleyan University. Heidi is the author of the comedic novel *Lala Pettibone's Act Two* (finalist, Foreword Reviews Book of the Year) and the sequel, *Lala Pettibone: Standing Room Only*. With Cristina Negrón and Deb Martin, Heidi writes *The Classics Slacker Reads . . .* series. Heidi and James Napoli (*The Official Dictionary of Sarcasm*) are co-hosts of the *Movies Not Movies* comedy podcast. Heidi is a contributor to the *Washington Independent Review of Books* and the *New York Journal of Books*.

Pat McGrath was born into a large Irish Catholic family in New York, where she was educated in the public school system. She finished her bachelor's degree at Trinity College in Hartford, Connecticut. Pat credits her attitude to an early start in New York and her evolution to her eclectic experiences. She is certified in feng shui, meditation instruction, Reiki, and spiritual counseling. Her focus is helping to guide women back to their innate sense of self-worth. You can find her at www.patmcgrathhealing.com.

Lara Scalzi Meek is a proud Nutmegger, born and raised in Connecticut. She is a graduate of the University of Connecticut, with a BA in English, a minor in Women's Studies, and a Creative Writing concentration. Lara currently lives in Oakland, California, with her husband, where she is a Bay Area performer, mother, and writer of fiction during nap times (the babies', not hers). She enjoys historic dive bars, coffee, reading, and costume opportunities.

Lisa Smith Molinari is the award-winning columnist behind "The Meat and Potatoes of Life," which appears weekly in *Stars and Stripes* and military community newspapers worldwide. Her book, *The Meat and Potatoes of Life: My True Lit Com* (2020 Elva Resa Publishing), is a hilariously readable sitcom based on the honest reality of Lisa's twenty-seven years as a US Navy wife and mother of three. Her book has received three national awards. Lisa is also a lawyer and cofounder of The Orion Military Scholarship Fund, Inc., a public charity. Lisa and her family live in Jamestown, Rhode Island.

Ebony Murphy-Root teaches middle school Humanities at Crossroads School for Arts & Sciences in Santa Monica and is the elected Southern California Class Representative for the 2021 cohort of Emerge California. She is an alumna of the University of Connecticut and the 2012 Campaign School at Yale and volunteers on the boards of Being Alive Los Angeles, a client-driven organization focusing on the mental health and wellness of people living with HIV and AIDS; NARAL Pro-Choice California; and Arts Alive, which offers music and performing arts classes to young artists from diverse backgrounds. Ebony recently trained with the Los Angeles African American Women's Public Policy Institute.

A Connecticut native, **Emily Parrow**'s decision to major in history stemmed from her love of storytelling. Her award-winning research has addressed topics ranging from Imperial Russian empresses to a formerly top-secret Cold War bunker, and in April 2021 she defended her MA thesis on nineteenth century Newport, Rhode Island's physical and social evolution. When not reading or writing, Emily enjoys thrifting, visiting coffee shops, and listening to podcasts and Emmylou Harris records. She is pursuing a career in the museum field and currently lives in Virginia.

A 2021 graduate of the University of Connecticut, **Faith Pease** earned a degree in Business with a concentration in Creative Writing. She took Professor Barreca's Modern British Literature class during her sophomore year and then took at least one course with Barreca every semester, including an independent study focused on creative writing. In addition to being a devoted writer and reader, Faith is an avid cook and recipe creator, delightedly serving up bons mots on her blog, *foodingwithfaith*. Faith is excited to be launching her post-grad professional career with TJX in Framingham, Massachusetts.

Sherry Pinamonti is a retired US Air Force officer and mother of three small children. She can identify both military aircraft and a full diaper at a glance. Sherry holds a BA in English from the University of Connecticut. She also holds a child on one hip, sticky toddler hands, and twenty expired Bed Bath & Beyond coupons in her purse.

Fiona Pitt-Kethley is the author of more than twenty books published by Chatto and Windus, Abacus, Peter Owen, Salt, and others. She lives in Spain with her husband the chess grandmaster, James Plaskett. They have a son, Alexander, and seven adopted feral cats. Her book on collecting minerals, *Washing Amethysts in the Bidet*, will be published by U P Publications this year. She is currently looking for publishers for new poetry collections and a novel.

Yvonne Ransel is a Midwest writer of essays—some humorous, some poignant—who is inspired by life's crazy, everyday events. She was a librarian, then a bar owner, now a librarian again. She survived the '60s, the millennium, and the years since as wife, mother, and now grandmother of six. She lives on the beautiful St. Joseph River in northern Indiana after graduating from Miami University of Ohio—a college established before Florida was a state—and earning her MLS at Indiana University. She is a contributor to two humor anthologies, *Feisty After 45* and *Laugh Out Loud*, and writes a monthly essay for her hometown newspaper, the *Elkhart Truth*.

Niloufar Rezai is a first-generation Persian-American who is passionate about teaching, and learning. Throughout her career, she has taught every age from preschool through college. As someone who has overcome obstacles—physical limitations as well as injustices in the form of microaggressions—she is sensitive to students' experiences and values each individual. She imparts to faculty teaching pre-service teachers the importance of considering each student's experience, needs, culture, and disposition in the classroom and beyond. Her son, Bijan, and daughter, Leila, are proud of their Persian background.

Teri Rizvi is the author of *One Heart with Courage: Essays and Stories* (Braughler Books, 2021). She founded and directs the Erma Bombeck Writers' Workshop at the University of Dayton, where she serves as Executive Director of Strategic Communications. She is co-editor of *Laugh Out Loud: 40 Women Humorists Celebrate Then and Now . . . Before We Forget* and *Sisters!*, a humor book celebrating the bond of sisters (and soul sisters), both published in conjunction with the workshop. Her essays and feature stories have appeared in *USA Today*, the *Christian Science Monitor*, *The Guardian*, and *University of Dayton Magazine*, among others.

Jennifer Few Rizzo has been published in the *Hartford Courant* for her narratives "The Loss of Karlonzo Taylor Is a Loss for Everyone" and "The Only Thing That'll Be Showing Is a Ring." Her piece "Better with Age" was also included in *Fast Funny Women*. She received a bachelor's degree in English and a master's in K–12 Special Education from the University of Connecticut and her 092 certification and Sixth Year Degree from Sacred Heart University. She has served as an adjunct professor at Bay Path University since 2016 and teaches in Vernon, Connecticut. She is devoted to social justice and equity in education and currently lives in Connecticut with her husband, two children, and two dogs.

Laura Rossi is a public relations expert, digital strategist, podcast producer, and published author. For three decades, Laura has led book publicity campaigns for best-selling authors as well as for national companies and brands in the lifestyle, non-profit, and art and design industries. Laura worked in-house at top publishers including Random House, Viking Penguin, and W. W. Norton before founding Laura Rossi Public Relations. Laura is the producer of *Parent Footprint with Dr. Dan*, an Exactly Right/My Favorite Murder network podcast. Laura Rossi is a contributor to several collections, including *Make Mine a Double, The Grateful Life, Fast Funny Women,* and *Fast Fierce Women*. Laura has appeared in the *New York Times, Psychology Today,* the *Chronicle of Higher Education,* the *Huffington Post,* and NPR's The Public's Radio. Laura volunteers as the Director of Publicity for the digital literary platform A Mighty Blaze. Follow Laura, @bookpgirl, on Instagram and Twitter.

Jennifer Sager is a public relations, communications, and organizational strategy professional; an avid reader, aspiring writer, passionate recycler, enthusiastic runner, and yogi. While she spends much of her days writing and organizing others, she continues to find small pockets of time to write for herself, a welcome and refreshing change of pace! Jennifer lives in Hartford, Connecticut, with her charming husband and their two smart, spirited children.

Amy Hartl Sherman is a writer, haiku poet, cartoonist, humorist, graduate of the University of Illinois, and retired flight attendant. Humor is her religion. It heals the soul.

Joan Seliger Sidney is Writer-in-Residence at the University of Connecticut's Center for Judaic Studies and Contemporary Jewish Life. Her books include *Body of Diminishing Motion: Poems and a Memoir* (CavanKerry), an Eric Hoffer Legacy finalist; *Bereft and Blessed* (AntrimHouse); and *The Way the Past Comes Back* (The Kutenai Press). Her flash essay, "I Married a Mathematician," appeared in *Fast Funny Women* (Woodhall Press). Joan's poems and essays have been published in many anthologies and literary journals. She has also translated French poems by Mireille Gansel, which have been nominated for a Pushcart Prize.

Cheyenne Smith is an emerging writer from Egg Harbor Township, New Jersey. Growing up, she was captivated by the art of storytelling. By age seven, Cheyenne knew that was the path for her. This fall, Cheyenne will be entering her senior year at the University of Connecticut. She is on track to getting a bachelor's degree in both English and Film Studies. In the future, she hopes to put her love of writing stories and watching films toward a career in screenwriting.

Meg Sommerfeld is a creative communications professional who has worked as a consultant to numerous foundations, universities, and nonprofit organizations. A former journalist for *Education Week* and the *Chronicle of Philanthropy*, she has a problem-solving mindset and a flair for transforming complex ideas into clear, compelling stories. Meg has a master's degree in Public Policy from the Kennedy School of Government and a bachelor's degree in History from Dartmouth College. She is an avid volunteer, reader, word game player, and the mom of two daughters. They are the sunshine in her life, and she aspires to be half as fierce as they are.

The Reverend **Jamie Spriggs** is the grateful pastor of First Baptist Church in Fall River, Massachusetts, which is known in the community as "the church that helps people." Jamie is especially grateful for meaningful, joy-filled work, because for seventeen previous years she was the 24/7 caregiver for her Alzheimer's-afflicted mother, who occupied the bulk of her time, resources, and attention. As the year since her mother's death has been a time of pandemic, Jamie has yet to explore who she is becoming after caregiving. Whatever else her future includes, it will continue to bring heron-seeking canoe trips in the late-afternoon sun.

Suzette Martinez Standring is a spirituality columnist for the *Patriot Ledger* (Massachusetts) and nationally syndicated (2008–2021). She teaches writing workshops based on her award-winning books, *The Art of Column Writing* and *The Art of Opinion Writing*, which are used in university journalism courses, including Johns Hopkins University. Since 2009, she hosts and produces a TV show about authors on cable TV, *It's All Write with Suzette*. Visit www.readsuzette.com, or email her at suzmar@comcast.net.

Named by *Bustle* as one of eight women writers to follow, **Tracy Strauss** is the author of the memoir *I Just Haven't Met You Yet*. Her essays have been published in *New York* magazine, *Glamour*, *O, the Oprah Magazine*, *Writer's Digest* magazine, *Poets & Writers* magazine, *Salon*, *Cognoscenti*, the *Southampton Review*, *HuffPost*, and others. The 2015 Writers Room of Boston Nonfiction Fellow and Former Essays Editor of *The Rumpus*, Tracy is a past winner of the Barbara Deming Memorial Fund Award for nonfiction. She teaches Writing (and Zumba) in Boston, where she lives with her dog, Beau, and her cat, Sam.

Leslie Morgan Steiner is the author of the *New York Times* best-selling memoir *Crazy Love*; the critically acclaimed anthology *Mommy Wars: Stay-at-Home and Career Moms Face Off on Their Choices, Their Lives, Their Families*; *The Baby Chase: How Surrogacy Is Transforming the American Family*; and her latest memoir, *The Naked Truth*, which explores female sexuality, self-esteem, and dating after fifty. She holds an undergraduate degree from Harvard College and an MBA from Wharton Business School. Her TED talks about domestic violence and the ethics of global surrogacy have been viewed by more than seven million people. Visit her at www.lesliebooks.com.

Victoria Sun is a graduate of the University of Connecticut. She is a recipient of the national silver medal from the Scholastic Art and Writing Awards in the Humor category. She is a contributing author of the *Connecticut Student Writings Project V. XXXVII* (2015) and *Nonwhite and Woman* (Woodhall Press, 2022).

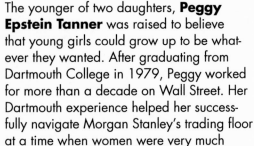

The younger of two daughters, **Peggy Epstein Tanner** was raised to believe that young girls could grow up to be whatever they wanted. After graduating from Dartmouth College in 1979, Peggy worked for more than a decade on Wall Street. Her Dartmouth experience helped her successfully navigate Morgan Stanley's trading floor at a time when women were very much in the minority. Peggy is happily married to David Tanner and is the proud mother of three sons. She is a serial board member and volunteer for numerous not-for-profit organizations. In her free time, she plays ice hockey with the New Canaan Mother Puckers.

Emily Toth, always a feminist activist, wrote her prizewinning dissertation (Johns Hopkins University) on Kate Chopin. She has spent a lifetime rediscovering, teaching, and celebrating women writers. She has created such courses as "Strong Women in Literature: Tough Cookies," "Food Writing," and "Women's Secrets." Her eleven published books include biographies of Chopin and Grace Metalious; a Civil War novel; and advice books for academics under the persona of "Ms. Mentor." She is a professor at Louisiana State University, an online columnist, and a speaker about women's lives, humor, gossip, and imagination. She sings in the Baton Rouge Rock 'n' Roll Chorus.

Debbie Turvey currently resides in Maplewood, New Jersey, with her husband, Tom, three children—Grace, Annie, and Nate—and their two dogs, Panda and Peanut. She is a proud graduate of the University of Connecticut and has spent her career working in children's books and as an author/illustrator booking agent.

Danielle Waring's first essay, "How I Survived Being Bullied," was published in the 2019 October *Hartford Courant*. Danielle lives in Connecticut with her husband, Paulo, and her fur-babies, Chewy and Ronin. Before she became an English teacher, Danielle helped found Greenwich's Off Center Stage Theater Company. At the University of Connecticut, when she wasn't cha-cha-cha-ing, she was privileged enough to have Professor Gina Barecca and earned her master's degree in Education/English. After college, Danielle took a comatose-cancer summer break and then earned her first teaching position in Stamford. You can email Danielle at dwaring@ stamfordct.gov.

Amy Whipple would prefer to write this bio in the first person, but apparently that's still not a thing people do. She is a Pittsburgh-based writer, a church secretary, and parent of the magnificent WD. She watches a lot of TV, eats ice cream every night, and is working on a book about advocacy, community, and twenty-first-century togetherness. She holds an MFA in Nonfiction Writing from the University of Pittsburgh, is the nonfiction co-editor of *K'in*, and her writing can be found in *Pittsburgh Magazine*, *VICE*, and *The Guardian*, among others. You should probably also know she's a delightful person.

Ryan E. Wiltzius is thirty-one years old and lives in Brooklyn, New York, with her most beloved companions: her high school sweetheart (now fiancé) and their boxer, Odin. She is an essayist and a poet to her core, though you can also find her tutoring and babysitting the children of BKLYN, wandering the streets attempting to cinematize everyday phenomena, and/or making music with her best friend for their band, Tender End. She never—ever—leaves home without a notebook.

Miranda Wright is a recent graduate of the University of Connecticut with a BFA concentrating in Illustration/Animation and a minor in English. Her artwork has been chosen for multiple scholarships, including the John S. Fawcett Illustration Award, the Cynthia Reeves Snow Watercolor Scholarship, and the Doudera Art Scholarship. She works as a book designer and aspires to be a novelist and illustrator. When not creating, Miranda spends her time reading, traveling, and watching movies. She lives in Connecticut with her family, two very loud birds, and their King Charles spaniel, Dash. Her artwork can be found on Instagram @miranda.sketches.

Mia Yanosy graduated from the University of Connecticut in May 2021 with a degree in English. She was a part of the Connecticut Poetry Circuit in the winter of 2021 and has a short story forthcoming in *Iron Horse Literary Review*.

About the Editor

Hailed as "smart and funny" by *People*, **Gina Barreca** was deemed a "feminist humor maven" by *Ms.* Her weekly columns are distributed by the Tribune Co. and she's written for most major publications, including *The New York Times*, *The Chronicle of Higher Education*, *Cosmopolitan*, and *The Harvard Business Review*. Board of Trustees Distinguished Professor at UCONN as well as winner of its highest award for excellence in teaching, Gina's written ten books including *If You Lean In, Will Men Just Look Down Your Blouse?*; *It's Not That I'm Bitter*; *Babes in Boyland: A Personal History of Coeducation in the Ivy League*; and the bestselling *They Used to Call Me Snow White But I Drifted*. You can find her in the Library of Congress or the makeup aisle at Walgreens. For more information, visit her at *ginabarreca.com*